Responding Well
to Domestic Abuse

Responding Well
to Domestic Abuse

Policy and Practice Guidance

2nd edition 2017

 CHURCH HOUSE PUBLISHING

© *The Archbishops' Council 2017*

Published in 2017 for the House of Bishops of the General Synod of the Church of England

Church House Publishing
Church House, Great Smith Street,
London, SW1P 3AZ.

ISBN 978 0 7151 1118 5

Email: copyright@churchofengland.org

For a downloadable electronic version of the full document for local, non-commercial use, please consult the Church of England website: www.churchofengland.org

British Library Cataloguing in Publication Data.
A catalogue record for this book is available from the British Library

Preface

Dear Colleagues,

In 2006 the Church of England produced the 'Responding to Domestic Abuse: Guidelines for those with Pastoral Responsibilities'. This was in response to a motion passed by the General Synod of the Church of England in July 2004:

'That this Synod, noting that domestic violence is regarded by the Home Office and the police as a crime:

(a) *view with extreme alarm the number of incidents being regularly reported, as being an unacceptable picture of suffering and abuse;*

(b) *call for national guidelines to be issued by the Archbishops' Council for those with pastoral care responsibilities, as to the appropriate relationship with both victims and perpetrators;*

(c) *recognise the special circumstances associated with domestic violence, and therefore the special needs of victims, in minority ethnic communities; and*

(d) *urge all dioceses to consider ways in which they could i) work in partnership with other agencies, co-operating sensitively with those serving minority communities, to provide the resources needed by victims and their families; ii) speak out against the evil of domestic violence; and iii) work for justice and safety in the homes of this nation.'*

The Church remains committed to those who have been survivors/victims of domestic abuse and to addressing the processes that lead to domestic abuse. Domestic abuse in all its forms is contrary to the will of God and an affront to human dignity. All need to play their part in preventing or halting it.

I hope that this updated practice guidance will help church communities address the issues in an informed way and be of use to anyone entrusted by victims, survivors or perpetrators to hear their story. In doing so, we acknowledge the excellent work that is already taking place in many churches, by many Christians and by those working in voluntary and statutory organisations and we are grateful for their help in drawing up this revised practice guidance.

Yours in Christ's fellowship,

+ Peter Bathand Wells

The Right Reverend Peter Hancock
Bishop of Bath and Wells
Lead Bishop on Safeguarding

Contents

Contributions

Thanks are owed to the Domestic Abuse Task Group (see below) for their contribution to the preparation of this practice guidance. 'Restored' have assisted with the re-drafting of this practice guidance, following a very comprehensive response to the consultation. Additional thanks go to the dioceses of Southwark and Canterbury for the use of some of their materials.

Karen Shooter	Lincolnshire Social Services – DV Services
Debbie Johnson	Diocesan Safeguarding Adviser, Lincoln
Morag Keane	Diocesan Safeguarding Adviser, Chichester
Duncan Sheppard	National Offender Management Service
Glenys Armstrong	Diocesan Safeguarding Adviser, Bath and Wells
Lucy Lord	Women's Aid
Mandy Marshall	Restored
Scilla Wallis	Supporter
Chris Hawkins	Clergy perspective
Paul Weatherstone	Policy lead DV in National Offender Management Service (NOMS)

Introduction

Aim

This document sets out the Church of England's Domestic Abuse Policy and the detailed practice guidance on how the Church of England will implement ts Domestic Abuse Policy. It supports the Church's commitment to address and respond effectively to domestic abuse both within its own community and wider society.

It replaces and updates 'Responding to Domestic Abuse; Guidelines for those with pastoral responsibilities 2006'.

The practice guidance is intended to raise awareness and to highlight some of the areas that need to be considered in making our churches safer places. To encourage churches to become places of safety where domestic abuse is taken seriously, victims/survivors are believed and respected and alleged or known perpetrators are challenged.

It aims to inform, direct and equip those working at a local level, not only those working in authorised ministries such as clergy, readers or pastoral assistants, but also those who may be entrusted by victims/survivors or alleged or known perpetrators to hear their story and who want to offer the most appropriate care.

Scope

This policy applies to all church bodies and officers.[1,2] Full understanding of, and adherence to, this policy should lead to a deepening in the understanding of, and respect for, the rights of children, young people and adults as people of faith in the life of the Church.

Under section 5 of the Safeguarding and Clergy Discipline Measure 2016,[3] all authorised clergy, bishops, archdeacons, licensed readers and lay workers, churchwardens and PCCs must have '**due regard**' to safeguarding guidance (sections 1, 2 and 3 of this document) issued by the House of Bishops (this will include both policy and practice guidance). A duty to have 'due regard' to

---

[1] Church Bodies, include parishes, dioceses, cathedrals, religious communities, theological training institutions, NCIs and other associated bodies. NCIs include The Archbishops' Council; Bishopthorpe Palace; The Church Commissioners; The Church of England Central Services; The Church of England Pensions Board; Lambeth Palace; National Society for Promoting Religious Education; Trustees of the Lambeth Palace Library. This policy will apply to the whole of the provinces of Canterbury and York (including the Diocese in Europe subject to local variations/modifications). There is also an expectation that the policy will apply to the Channel Islands and Sodor and Man unless there is specific local legislation in a jurisdiction that would prevent adoption.

[2] A "Church Officer" is anyone appointed/elected by or on behalf of the Church to a post or role, whether they are ordained or lay, paid or unpaid

[3] The Safeguarding and Clergy Discipline Measure 2016 applies to the whole of the provinces of Canterbury and York (including the Diocese in Europe subject to local variations/modifications), with the exception of the Channel Islands and Sodor and Man. In order to extend the 2016 Measure to the Channel Islands or Sodor and Man legislation will need to be passed by the relevant island jurisdictions in accordance with section 12 of that Measure.

guidance means that the person under the duty is not free to disregard it but is required to follow such guidance unless there are cogent reasons for not doing so ('cogent' for this purpose means clear, logical and convincing). Failure by clergy to comply with the duty imposed by the 2016 Measure may result in disciplinary action.

The Ecclesiastical Insurance Group has made it clear that their insurance cover is only valid where House of Bishops safeguarding policy and practice guidance is being followed.

Outline

Section 1 outlines the Church of England's Policy on Domestic Abuse. Section 2 outlines the procedure for responding to domestic abuse and Section 3 outlines the training requirements. This is supported by 9 Appendices which provide good practice reference material and templates.

This is not an all-inclusive resource, excellent resources that cover this subject more thoroughly can be found in Appendix 9. The guidance recognises that often the Church's role involves supporting victims/survivors, empowering them to seek professional care from the relevant agencies. The Church can also support alleged or known perpetrators of abuse, by encouraging them to recognise their personal needs and seek appropriate help or by reinforcing what is being done by others to help them to take responsibility for and address their abusive attitudes and behaviour. This may include referring individuals to a programme for alleged or known perpetrators of domestic abuse.

Additional associated House of Bishops Practice Guidance documents supplement this practice guidance[4] and are referenced in this policy.

Building on this, church bodies may provide additional local procedures and guidance in line with the House of Bishops policy and practice guidance.

Where to find the policy

It will be distributed via email to all dioceses, cathedrals and other Church bodies. The most up to date version of the policy, model templates and the associated practice guidance, will always be available on the Church of England website.[5]

News of updates will be included in information circulated by the National Safeguarding Team.

Relevant information will be updated online, where the policy and associated practice guidance can be downloaded easily for local use, so that it is not necessary to supply large quantities of printed papers, which can become out of date all too quickly.

For those who do not have access to the internet, hard copies of the policy and associated documents can be supplied via their Diocesan Safeguarding Team or via Church House Publishing, on request.

Please note that the aim will be to move to a full electronic manual in 2017.

---

4 Safeguarding Policy Statements & Practice Guidance
5 Safeguarding Policy Statements & Practice Guidance

1.　Policy

> *Please note:* **You are reminded that the 'due regard' duty under section 5 of the Safeguarding and Clergy Discipline Measure 2016 applies.**

1.1　Context

The Church is committed to those who have been victims and survivors of domestic abuse.[6] Domestic abuse in all its forms is contrary to the will of God and an affront to human dignity. All need to play their part in preventing or halting it.

There is growing awareness in society of the extent of domestic abuse and recognition that domestic abuse is a crime, not a private matter to be kept in the family or community. This has resulted in amendments to legislation (see Appendix 2 for a summary of the legal context) and improved responses and interventions by police, housing and other statutory or voluntary agencies designed to improve safety, encourage partnership working and provide increased support to victims and perpetrators. Many of these agencies have been extremely supportive of the development of this guidance and are keen to work with the Church to support survivors and reduce the incidence of domestic abuse. We recognise that the Church is one institution in a network of many that must play its part in recognising and referring on cases of domestic abuse to those with statutory responsibility. Progress has been made in many dioceses in developing relationships with statutory and voluntary agencies working to address domestic abuse and this approach is recommended for all dioceses and parishes.

For the Church, support of survivors and response to alleged or known perpetrators of domestic abuse must be considered primarily as a safeguarding issue and also in the wider context of good pastoral care.

In July 2004 the General Synod of the Church of England passed a motion in relation to the Church's commitment to tackle domestic violence.

In addition the Anglican Communion resolutions 15:7 and 16:2, 3 provide a context for the Church to address issues of gender justice and domestic abuse.

In February 2014, the General Synod approved the following motion on gender-based violence:

'That this Synod, believing that all people are made in the image of God and that all forms of violence based on gender represent *an abuse and violation* of that image:

---

[6] Please see Appendix 1 for a definition of domestic abuse

- Affirm work already undertaken in dioceses, deaneries, parishes and Church of England schools in raising awareness and caring for survivors of gender-based violence in all our diverse communities;

- Support measures to bring alleged or known perpetrators to account and provide support for changed lifestyles;

- Encourage boys and men to stand against gender-based violence;

- Commend Anglican Consultative Council Resolution 15:7 on preventing and eliminating gender-based violence to dioceses, deaneries and parishes and urge them to seek practical approaches to its implementation.'

1.2   Our theological approach

When considering theology and domestic abuse we have to realise that religious or spiritual factors are central to the victim's understanding and response. His/her own faith and the support of Church can be vital in helping the healing process, while a lack of understanding regarding the Biblical perspective on abusive relationships by the victim or those he/she turns to for spiritual guidance and support can add to the emotional, physical and financial hurdles already faced.

The basis of our theological approach is summarised as follows:

- Human beings are created in the divine image to live in relationships of love, respect and mutual self-giving. This should be reflected in how intimate relationships are conducted.

- Tragically, the corruption of human nature which Christian theology names 'sin' means that the mutual dependence and shared vulnerability which are inseparable from intimacy can instead become the vehicle through which one person can inflict profound hurt, damage and abuse upon another.

- The pattern of living that is revealed through Jesus in his relationships with others entails that abuse of any kind is contrary to the will of God and an affront to human dignity. This entails a heavy responsibility upon the Church and its members to do everything possible to prevent or halt it.

- The good news of Christ promises God's redeeming presence and power in situations of pain and suffering. Through rejection of patterns of violence, and support of those who have been abused, the Church is called to be a vehicle of God's work of healing for both survivors and alleged or known perpetrators of abuse.

- The Church is committed to doing justice to the truth about God and human beings that is revealed in the Christian Gospel.

A summary of Biblical verses that have been used to justify abuse and more helpful interpretations of these verses is given in Appendix 3.

1.3   Church of England Policy on Domestic Abuse

The Church of England is committed to raising awareness about domestic abuse and its impact on individuals, children, the wider family and community.

It will work to ensure that:

- The safety of individuals suffering abuse or seeking help is the first priority, and to be aware of the need for confidentiality within the bounds of good safeguarding practice;

- Teaching and worship reflects awareness-raising about domestic abuse, uses appropriate language and says clearly that domestic abuse is wrong;

- Inappropriate behaviour is challenged, this needs to be done in an extremely careful way, in a way that does not place any individual including a victim at increased risk.

- Clergy and clergy spouses have the same access to support and resources as others who are experiencing domestic abuse. In addition the Diocesan Bishop will appoint a Bishop's Visitor[7] whose role is to support the clergy or clergy spouse at the time of the breakdown of the relationship, and for as long as possible after, as required.

It is committed to all church bodies:

- Adopting and publishing a local policy on domestic abuse, including who to contact if there are concerns;

- Having clear procedures in place to respond to concerns about domestic abuse in line with Responding to Domestic Abuse Practice Guidance and Responding to Serious Safeguarding Concerns Against Church Officers Practice Guidance.

- Ensuring signage is in place in local venues to demonstrate that your church or setting is willing to talk with everyone about domestic abuse and how to access support;

- Appointing a named individual who has responsibility for domestic abuse and violence and who is a point of contact for any advice and support. This may be the DSA, PSO or the nominated safeguarding lead;

- Training those in leadership positions, safeguarding roles and with pastoral roles on domestic abuse;

- Discussing domestic abuse and violence in appropriate contexts such as marriage preparation, youth groups, ordinand training and in church settings;

- Organising and promoting training and awareness-raising sessions;

- Working with Statutory agencies and other support bodies. Supporting and publicising their work.

---

[7] See section 2.5.1

1.4   What do you need to do in a diocese?

Drawing on the policy statement, the table below summarises what a diocese needs to have in place (this can be adapted for other church bodies):

Summary guidance on domestic abuse for dioceses

Do:

- Adopt and publish a domestic abuse statement, including who to contact if there are concerns (see Appendix 4 for a template Diocesan Statement);

- Appoint a named individual who is a point of contact for any advice and support for parishes and other church bodies, as appropriate. This may be the DSA;

- Have clear procedures in place to respond to concerns about domestic abuse in line with Section 3 and Responding to Serious Safeguarding Concerns against Church Officers Practice Guidance;[8]

- Monitor all concerns in relation to domestic abuse allegations and concerns against church officers in the diocese;

- Provide support to parishes to implement the domestic abuse policy and practice guidance;

- Appoint a Bishop's Visitor and ensure that all clergy and their partners know how to access support;

- Deliver a domestic abuse training programme for those in leadership positions, safeguarding and pastoral roles in the diocese and parishes;

- Work in partnership with other specialist agencies.

Recommended good practice:

Offer additional resources and materials to parishes such as materials for raising awareness sessions, etc.

---

[8] Safeguarding Policy Statements & Practice Guidance

1.5   What do you need to do in a parish?

Drawing on the policy statement, the table below summarises what a parish needs to have in place (this can be adapted for other church bodies):

Summary guidance on domestic abuse for parishes

Do:

- PCC to agree a parish domestic abuse statement including who to contact if there are concerns (see Appendix 5 for template Parish Statement);

- Appoint a named individual who is a point of contact for any advice and support. This may be the Parish Safeguarding Officer (PSO);

- Follow the process on how to respond to concerns about domestic abuse (see Section 2). *If parishes are in any doubt as to what action to take they should refer to the Diocesan Safeguarding Adviser (DSA).*

- Support those in leadership positions, pastoral and safeguarding roles to engage in Diocesan domestic abuse training.

- Consider the best place to display the domestic abuse statement including information about helplines and local services.

- Discuss domestic abuse in appropriate contexts such as marriage preparation (see Appendix 8 for good practice guidance).

- Challenge inappropriate comments and behaviour by church members.

Recommended good practice:

- Encourage leaders and those who preach to speak against domestic abuse in teaching, sermons, prayers and parish magazines – remember that many of the congregation may have a personal experience.

- Offer some awareness raising activities e.g. invite speakers from local domestic abuse agencies, organise an activity around 25 November (the International Day for the Elimination of Violence Against Women).

- Consider including activities around healthy relationships within activities for children and young people.

- Develop links with any local domestic abuse organisations.

- Organise courses in parenting and confidence-building.

---

2.   The Church's Response to Domestic Abuse

> **Please note:** **You are reminded that the 'due regard' duty under section 5 of the Safeguarding and Clergy Discipline Measure 2016 applies.**

2.1 Responding to victims/survivors

> It is sometimes tempting to minimize the survivor's experiences. After all (we might wrongly reason), we've all been in arguments, so if they can't cope, then it's their problem. Yet an abusive relationship is not about an ordinary, everyday argument in which both people have a bit of a yell and then make up. It is very different indeed and often involves repeated behaviour. We must guard against deciding which abusive behaviour is worth bothering with, and which is not. We must offer help and support to all who ask for and need it.
>
> *Responding to Domestic Abuse: Guidelines for Those with Pastoral Responsibilities*, 2006 (p.24) Church of England. Archbishops' Council.

The guidance below aims to assist you in responding to people disclosing abuse. If you feel ill-equipped to deal with the situation please contact the DSA for advice and guidance. The safety of children and victims is paramount. All actions should carefully consider the risk to their, and your, safety. Telephone calls, holding information about support services for domestic abuse, the use of texts and emails and accessing relevant websites all create potential risks for those experiencing abuse.

For information on the statutory definition of abuse, its prevalence and effects, and how to recognise both victims/survivors and alleged perpetrators please see Appendix 1. This also includes information on specialist types of domestic abuse.

Initial disclosure

If a victim discloses abuse, the following factors are important:

- Most victims/survivors want to be asked. If you are able to broach the subject, your offer of help could be the first step in enabling them to seek help; e.g. 'How are things at home?' and if it becomes appropriate, 'Is anyone hurting you?'

- Do try wherever possible to talk in a safe, private place where you will not be interrupted, or arrange to talk again (but someone in distress may start talking anywhere).

- Do try to make it clear that complete confidentiality cannot be guaranteed, depending on the nature of what is disclosed. Whilst you might respect an individual's right to confidentiality this cannot be guaranteed i.e. when someone is being hurt and a criminal offence has been committed, someone is in danger, or when children are involved.

- Do take plenty of time to listen and believe what they say. If they sense disbelief they may be discouraged from speaking again.

Immediate action

- Do dial 999 (112 in Europe) if you are witnessing a violent incident or if the person needs medical care. If the victim is in immediate danger, the police should be called. Be aware that intervention may heighten risk, but it is important to explore how to ensure people are safe.

- The safety of children is paramount. If children are involved, a referral to Children's Service needs to be made in addition to calling the police; if possible, encourage the victim to make the referral themselves, perhaps supporting them through the process. The DSA will also need to be informed.

Your response to the disclosure

- Do be sensitive to people's backgrounds and cultures and check your own and their understanding of how the cultural issues affect them. Ask them about what support is available to them from friends and family.

- Do affirm the strength and courage it takes to have survived the abuse and even more to talk about it.

- Do encourage them to seek professional help from a local domestic abuse service who will be able to offer practical safety planning advice, even if they do not want to leave their home. In addition give information about national specialist helplines and websites, as required (see Appendix 9).

- Do express concern for their safety and immediate welfare. Do they have somewhere to stay?

- Do ask about the children and their safety and welfare. You may need to persuade them to report any concerns to children's social care. You have no option but to do so if you have received information that a child is at risk.

- Do encourage them to focus on their own needs, something they may not have been able to do since the abuse began but which is critical in helping them to change their situation.

- Do reassure them that, whatever the circumstances, abuse is not justified and not their fault.

- Do ask them what they want from you and the parish. Offer help which is in response to their needs and preferences and which lets them keep in control.

Record keeping and follow up

Appendix 7 covers issues of confidentiality and data protection. Summary guidance is as follows:

- Do check if it is all right to contact them at home before doing so. Ask them what their preferred means of contact is and confirm that this is safe.

- Do keep information confidential and as a general rule only share with informed consent where appropriate and if possible, respect the wishes of those who do not give consent to share confidential information. You should note that it may still be possible to share confidential information without consent if, in your judgement, it is necessary and proportionate to do so (i.e. there is a good reason), such as where the safety of the victim or (an) other(s) may be at risk. Always keep a record of your decision and the reasons why you decided to share (or not). If in doubt contact the DSA and the Diocesan Registrar.

- Do make a brief objective note of date, facts and context of what you have been told but keep your opinions separate. This should be kept in strict confidence but could be useful in any future prosecution (see Safeguarding Records: Joint Practice Guidance for the Church of England and the Methodist Church (2015)).

- You must **share the incident with someone who is qualified within 24 hours** and can support you to help you to think through the issues and action. This may be the DSA or local safeguarding officer/lead.

- Do seek advice from the DSA or local safeguarding officer/lead to review the safety and risk issues in relation to the alleged perpetrator if they are in the same church. There may need to be a risk assessment and 'safeguarding agreement' put in place in line with House of Bishops practice guidance.[9] This work needs be undertaken in consultation with the DSA.

- Victim safety planning should be conducted by a professional, ideally from a domestic abuse service or a statutory agency. There may be an occasion when a victim wishes to discuss their safety with you. It is essential that you seek advice from a DSA before entering into detailed safety planning discussions. This planning would normally be guided by a safety planning format (see Appendix 6) and careful consideration should be given to where and how such information is provided and kept by the victim, to avoid being accessed by the perpetrator.

- If the **alleged perpetrator is a church officer** you must talk to the DSA and follow the House of Bishops practice guidance on responding to serious safeguarding concerns in relation to church officers.[10]

- **Do not give information about the victim's whereabouts to the perpetrator or to others who might pass information on to the perpetrator.** Do not discuss with the parish council/other members of a congregation who might inadvertently pass information on to the perpetrator.

---

[9] Safeguarding Policy Statements & Practice Guidance
[10] Safeguarding Policy Statements & Practice Guidance

- When victims are leaving a controlling perpetrator, they often have to leave with nothing and have access to very limited financial support. Consider how your church can provide practical support to survivors.

Key telephone numbers for sources of help

- National Domestic Violence Helpline: 0808 2000 247

- Legal support (National Centre for Domestic Violence):
  0844 8044 999 – provides a free, fast, emergency injunction service for victims of domestic abuse

- Male victims (Respect): 0808 801 0327

- Helpline for domestic abuse in same sex relationships:
  0800 999 5428

2.1.1 Disclosure flowchart

It is recognised that it can be difficult to make a referral, which can be with or without the permission of the victim. Local Authority Social Care Departments are aware of the issues and sensitivities in relation to domestic abuse, and will ensure that they operate with professionalism and an awareness of the situation. Nevertheless, it is important that they are aware of the information concerning domestic abuse, so that they can act on it appropriately. It is not the role of the Church, nor anyone employed within the Church, to investigate the issues and incidents – only social care and the police have these statutory powers.

Please follow this process when you become aware of an incident of domestic abuse and violence.

Please note this flowchart will be made available as a separate document on the Church of England website

A disclosure flowchart

Respect

- Believe the victim
- Do not ask for proof
- Assure the victim it is not their fault
- Reassure that confidentiality will be maintained but explain its boundaries

Is there an immediate risk of harm?

Yes →

Call the police

Discuss your concerns with the DSA

No ↓

Are there children involved?

Yes →

Discuss your concerns with the DSA, refer to Children's Services

No ↓

Further action requested?

No

Your time has been well spent. The victim will know that they can return to you for further help, that they have been believed and that they are not in the wrong.

You might be able to offer other opportunities to come and talk.

You cannot make the victim of domestic violence or abuse take any action. The most you might be able to do is listen and provide information.

Ensure you record what you have been told as a safeguarding concern, make a record of your actions and/or advice. Date the record and keep it confidentially.

Yes

Outline realistic options – police, Women's Aid, refuge, safe house.

Supply appropriate information, leaflets and contact numbers.

Make a referral on the victim's behalf (with their permission) if that is wanted.

Ensure you make a record of what you have been told as a safeguarding concern, note your actions and who you have sought advice from. Date the record and keep it confidentially.

2.2 Responding to alleged or known perpetrators

The Church has an important role in challenging inappropriate behaviour. This can, however, lead to increased risks for both the victim and the person who challenges the alleged or known perpetrator. This needs to be done in an extremely careful way, i.e. one that does not place a victim at increased risk. Factors to consider include:

- Ensuring that the victim is at the highest priority in terms of safety and wellbeing, and that any action is victim/survivor centred.

- If the alleged perpetrator is to be met, ensuring that it is in a public place, and that there are others in the meeting.

- Maintaining an awareness of the danger that the alleged perpetrator may pose to you, and ensuring that you and others are safe.

- You must **share the incident with a properly trained professional within 24 hours** who can support you to help you to think through the issues and actions. This may be the DSA or local safeguarding officer/lead. There may need to be a risk assessment and 'safeguarding agreement' put in place in line with House of Bishops practice guidance.[11] This work needs be undertaken in consultation with the DSA.

- If the **alleged perpetrator is a church officer** you must talk to the DSA and follow the House of Bishops practice guidance on responding to serious safeguarding concerns in relation to church officers.[12]

- Co-operating and working with the statutory authorities ensuring that information is only given to them and not to the alleged perpetrator concerning the victim.

- Sharing information about helplines and services.

Record keeping and follow up

Please see the previous section on 'record keeping and follow up' above. Additional guidance in relation to responding to alleged or known perpetrators is as follows.

Do try to make it clear that complete confidentiality cannot be guaranteed. Whilst you might respect an individual's right to confidentiality this cannot be guaranteed. Information has to be shared without consent when someone is being hurt, a criminal offence has been committed and/or a child or adult is at risk. If you are unsure whether or not to share information contact your Diocesan Safeguarding Adviser.

Do seek advice from a DSA or local safeguarding officer/lead if the alleged perpetrator threatens self-harm, as they may require urgent support.

Appendix 7 covers issues of confidentiality and data protection.

These are some actions to avoid in responding to alleged or known perpetrators:

- Do not collude with, excuse or minimise their behaviour.

---

[11] Safeguarding Policy Statements & Practice Guidance
[12] Safeguarding Policy Statements & Practice Guidance

- Do not meet with them alone and in private. Meet in a public place or in the church with several other people around.

- Do not try to investigate or offer/provide treatment. Only those professionally trained should discuss any issues formally with them.

- Do not provide a character witness in any proceedings and be involved in any processes which may seem as if the Church supports their position. Do not advocate for the perpetrator.

2.3 Additional guidance for clergy and licensed lay ministers

Responding to victims

- Do help the victim/survivor with any religious concerns.[13]

- Do emphasise that the marriage covenant is broken by the violence from their partner.

- **Do not pursue couples' counselling/mediation with them and their partner if you are aware that there is violence in the relationship.**

- Do assure them of God's love and presence.

- Do pray with them.

- Don't encourage them to forgive the alleged perpetrator and/or take them back.

Responding to perpetrators

- Do address any religious rationalisations they may offer or questions they may have.

- Do not allow them to use religious excuses for their behaviour.

- Do name the abuse as their problem, not the victim's/survivor's. Tell them that only they can stop it and seek assistance.

- **Do not pursue couples' counselling/mediation with them and their partner if you are aware that there is violence in the relationship.**

- Do not be taken in by his 'conversion' experience. If it is genuine, it will be a tremendous resource as they proceed with accountability. If it is phony, it is only another way to manipulate you and the system and maintain control of the process to avoid accountability.

- Do pray with them.

- Do assure them of your support in this endeavour.

Please see the FAOC paper on 'Forgiveness and Reconciliation' for further information.[14]

Perpetrator programmes

The attitudes that underpin domestic abuse are often deeply-rooted and difficult to change. Some success has been achieved through Domestic Violence Intervention Programmes for alleged or known perpetrators. These are extended

---

[13] A helpful book is 'KEEPING THE FAITH: GUIDANCE FOR CHRISTIAN WOMEN FACING ABUSE' Marie. M. Fortune
[14] This paper is still to be published at the time of publishing this document

(often six to nine months) one to one or group-based sessions which challenge the attitudes and behaviours of alleged or known perpetrators. Parallel groups may be organised for their partners to ensure that they are held to account.

Attendance at a perpetrator programme is often mandated by a court but it is possible in some parts of the country for men to self-refer to such programmes. Contact Respect (http://respect.uk.net/) or local authority for more details of local provision.

2.4   Pastoral issues

There are real issues for parishes where both parties continue to attend church. Parishes need to be aware of any legal restrictions around those perpetrating abuse and ensure these are not undermined. They need to consider how to support both parties safely, noting that the vicar cannot support both individuals. If they need further advice in relation to providing support they should contact the Diocesan Safeguarding Adviser.

If the victim/survivor or perpetrator is a member of the clergy, please talk urgently to the Diocesan Safeguarding Adviser to review the action required to ensure safety and the appropriate response (see section 2.5.2 below).

There is also the opportunity to form pastoral teams in order to provide emotional and pastoral support to those who are affected by domestic abuse. Training and awareness raising sessions should be available to the teams. These teams can consist of those who are available to support victims, a pastoral element, a trainer, and the safeguarding adviser in the parish and/or diocese/cathedral. The focus of the team is to ensure that there is support to victims/survivors within the church and that policies and practice guidance have been adopted. There may be a long-term need to provide pastoral support for survivors of domestic abuse, including support to couples when one or both parties have experienced abuse in a previous relationship.

2.5   Clergy and domestic abuse

If the partner of an ordained person, or an ordained person, discloses abuse, they must be treated in exactly the same way as any other victim. Clergy and clergy spouses must have the same access to support and resources as others who are experiencing domestic abuse.

If a member of the clergy or clergy partner who lives in church housing has decided to leave the relationship, they are likely to need alternative housing. Every Diocesan Bishop is advised to appoint a Bishop's Visitor for the victim/survivor of abuse, be they a member of the clergy or clergy spouse (see below). They may also consider appointing someone to offer pastoral support to an alleged perpetrator if they are a member of the clergy.

Clergy may see marital breakdown as a failure of their ordination vows and therefore be particularly vulnerable to staying in abusive relationships for many years. In such situations, dioceses should not put fear of scandal above the safety of vulnerable people. Clergy should expect to be believed by their Bishop when disclosing abuse, and supported should they wish to separate or divorce. An assessment should also be made of the likely risk to any children. At a most basic level, the survivor and family should be offered all reasonable steps to keep safe should they separate from the perpetrator (for example changing locks on the clergy housing). Clergy who are survivors should not be threatened with losing their post or housing in the event of divorce as this could create intolerable stress for the family and lead to people staying in dangerous situations. In such cases, the Church is compounding the abuse and colluding with the perpetrator. Counselling should be made available if requested for the survivor and any children.

2.5.1 Bishops' Visitors

The role of a visitor is to:

- Support the victim/survivor of abuse be they a member of the clergy or clergy spouse at the time of the breakdown of the marriage, and for as long as possible after, as the victim/spouse needs;

- Listen to, give information and represent the needs of the victim/survivor in the subsequent church and statutory enquiries, and help them think about next steps;

- Identify with the victim/survivor any additional pastoral needs e.g. therapeutic or other needs they have, and suggest how these may be best met, seeking advice from the DSA as required, including recommendations for payment of any required counselling;

- Record meetings or contact they have with the victim/survivor and passing on relevant information to the DSA as appropriate.

The visitor has a duty to disclose so as not to affect any investigation; it is important to recognise and to acknowledge that where others may still be at risk statutory agencies may need to be informed.

Both male and female visitors need to be available to accommodate individual needs and choice.

The frequency of contact between the visitor and the survivor needs to be agreed and under constant review in liaison with the survivor, the Bishop and the DSA. While in some cases it might be right for the visitor to remain in contact, there are also times when the individual should be referred to another person for counselling or other therapeutic care. The frequency and time limit of these sessions should be agreed between the survivor, Bishop and DSA. The question of whether the visitor also remains in touch will require careful thought, consultation and agreement with the Bishop and DSA. At all times it needs to be clear who is responsible for what.

Experience and skills

The key attributes of the visitor will be:

- Ability to listen;
- Ability to manage sensitive and difficult information;
- Ability to identify when a person may require more specialist support;
- Capacity to understand issues of confidentiality;
- Awareness and experience of supporting victims/survivors of domestic abuse;
- Awareness of how the Church works.

Training

The visitors will need domestic abuse training (see section 3).

2.5.2   Alleged perpetrator who is a member of the clergy

They must be treated in exactly the same way as any other alleged perpetrator (see section 2.2).

In addition under section 30 of the Clergy Discipline Measure 2003 (CDM), a priest who is

- convicted of any offence in England or elsewhere and is imprisoned (including a suspended sentence); or

- is convicted of an offence on indictment in England or Wales; or

- has a decree of divorce or an order of judicial separation made against him/her following a finding of adultery, behaviour in such a way that the petitioner cannot reasonably be expected to live with the respondent, or desertion and, in the case of divorce, the decree has been made absolute

- may be removed from office and/or prohibited from exercising any functions as a priest (whether for life or for a fixed term).[15]

Where a priest or deacon is being considered for appointment to a post and that person currently holds, or most recently held, a post in another diocese, the bishop of the 'receiving' diocese should apply to the bishop of the 'sending' diocese for a combined Reference and Current Status Letter in the form approved by the House of Bishops (hereafter in these notes called 'the Bishop's Reference'). The same procedure should apply when a retired priest or deacon applies for permission to officiate in a diocese other than that in which his or her confidential personal file ('blue file') is held.

Part B of the Bishop's Reference should include information relating to any concerns about safeguarding (paragraph 6). Safeguarding concerns could relate (but are not limited) to the protection of children, young people and adults from physical, emotional and/or sexual abuse, neglect or domestic violence. Even when the police have decided not to pursue an investigation, or the Crown Prosecution Service has declined to prosecute, any potential risk should still be assessed. If there is any relevant history, the bishop should consult the Diocesan Safeguarding Adviser before completing Part B.

Under the Data Protection Act 1998, the person about whom a Bishop's Reference is given will be entitled to ask to see it once it is in the hands of the receiving bishop. The Bishop's Reference should therefore, as a general rule, be expressed in a way that enables it to be shared with the priest or deacon concerned, and such sharing is recommended as a matter of good practice. However, some information may be exempt from disclosure, such as information that reveals the identity of a third party or information that may prejudice the prevention or detection of a crime or the capture or prosecution of an offender.

---

[15] Also in this list is a priest who is included in a barred list (i.e. in relation to children or vulnerable adults). The bishop has the power to do this outside the normal complaints procedure but must consult the President of Tribunals first and the respondent can make representations. For further information contact the Diocesan Registrar.

Therefore, advice should be sought from the Diocesan Registrar prior to sharing the information.

2.6 Mediation

Mediation is a specialist ministry which needs to be undertaken by trained experts. In order for mediation to work and to not make situations worse the parties involved must have equal power and must share some common vision of resolution. **It is not recommended that mediation is undertaken in cases of domestic abuse.** Mediation is an option or alternative to the civil law remedies in these cases and can, if used in an inappropriate manner, be a highly dangerous practice and increase the risk of harm to the victim.

A case study: Andrew and Jody

Andrew is separated from his wife, Jody, who had called the police and Andrew was arrested after an incident of domestic abuse. Charges were pressed and he was found guilty and given a community service order. Andrew is living apart from Jody. The couple have two children aged 6 and 8, both of whom live with Jody. Andrew wants to be reconciled with his wife and with the church of which they are both long-standing members. He has come to the vicarage to discuss this with the vicar, whom he asks to run an informal 'truth and reconciliation' meeting for anyone in the church who wants to come, in which he can explain what he has done, how sorry he is and how he is desperate to be reintegrated into his two homes – his domestic home and his spiritual home. He is currently not attending church.

Considerations in responding

The vicar needs to seek advice and support from the DSA in how best to respond.

The vicar needs to check out Andrew's motives: in approaching the vicar, who knows them both, Andrew might be seen as manipulating the vicar to support him, with the prime motive of reconciliation with his wife. What evidence is there of his repentance, and the steps he has taken to change his behaviour? How are his spiritual needs currently being met?

Any consideration of reconciliation with Jody must be in the context of assessing risk to her and risk to their children, and can only be considered if Jody is also willing to consider a conciliation process.

The vicar should not get involved in any conciliation between them as this is specialist work and needs to be undertaken by an independent agency equipped for the purpose. The vicar can signpost Andrew to such agencies.

The vicar can discuss with Andrew repentance and forgiveness by God, and arrange for him to receive spiritual care. This would be most appropriately offered by someone not known to either of them.

The vicar needs to be aware of boundaries of confidentiality, and should not be passing information from Andrew to Jody or vice versa. By so doing, not only may he lose the trust of one or the other, but he may be putting Jody at further risk.

The vicar should take care not to put the sanctity of marriage over the safety of vulnerable people.

2.7   Multi-agency response to domestic abuse

2.7.1 Independent Domestic Violence Advisors

Independent Domestic Violence Advisors (IDVAs) help keep victims and their children safe from harm from violent partners or family. Serving as a victim's primary point of contact, IDVAs normally work with their clients from the point of crisis, to assess the level of risk. They:

- discuss the range of suitable options;

- develop plans for immediate safety – including practical steps for victims to protect themselves and their children;

- develop plans for longer-term safety;

- represent their clients at the MARAC (see below);

- help apply sanctions and remedies available through the criminal and civil courts, including housing options.

These plans address immediate safety, including practical steps for victims to protect themselves and their children, as well as longer-term solutions. 80% of IDVAs are employed by voluntary agencies; the rest are in the public sector.

The DSA may refer to the IDVA service for support for high risk victims.

2.7.2 Multi-Agency Risk Assessment Conferences

- A Multi-Agency Risk Assessment Conference (MARAC) is a local, multi-agency victim-focused meeting where information is shared on the highest risk cases of domestic abuse between different statutory and voluntary sector agencies. Anyone can refer a case to a MARAC. Parishes would not normally expect to be involved in MARACs directly, but can refer a case through the DSA.

The MARAC aims to:

- share information to increase the safety, health and wellbeing of victims/survivors, adults and their children;

- determine whether the alleged perpetrator poses a significant risk to any particular individual or to the general community;

- construct jointly and implement a risk management plan that provides professional support to all those at risk and that reduces the risk of harm;

- reduce repeat victimisation;

- improve agency accountability; and

- improve support for staff involved in high-risk domestic abuse cases.

The agencies invited should be any that have a role to play in the victim and any children's safety, therefore the DSA may be invited to attend a MARAC to discuss safeguarding issues for the church.

2.7.3 Multi-Agency Public Protection Arrangements (MAPPA)

The Criminal Justice Act 2003 ('CJA 2003') provides for the establishment of
Multi-Agency Public Protection Arrangements ('MAPPA') in each of the 42
criminal justice areas in England and Wales. These are designed to protect the
public, including previous victims of crime, from serious harm by sexual and
violent offenders. They require the local criminal justice agencies and other
bodies dealing with offenders to work together in partnership in dealing with
these offenders.

MAPPA is not a statutory body in itself but it is a mechanism through which
agencies can better discharge their responsibilities and protect the public in a
co-ordinated manner. Although, generally, it is the statutory agencies that are
involved in the MAPPA, a DSA may be invited to attend a MAPPA to discuss
safeguarding issues for the church in managing a perpetrator.

2.7.4 Domestic Homicide Reviews

Domestic Homicide Reviews (DHR(s)) were established under section 9
of the Domestic Violence, Crime and Victims Act 2004.

The Secretary of State can direct that a DHR is carried out when a person
has been killed as a result of domestic violence. It attempts to identify what
happened, and what needs to change to reduce risk in the future. The
government guidance[16] notes that domestic violence and abuse which results
in the death of the victim is often not a first attack and is likely to have been
preceded by psychological and emotional abuse. Many people and agencies
may have known of the incidents, for instance: neighbours may have heard
violent arguments; doctors may have seen injuries; the police may have attended
residences; there may have been previous prosecutions and/or injunctions etc.
Serious injury and homicide in domestic violence and abuse cases can sometimes
be preventable if agencies intervene early. Therefore, it follows that local agencies
should have adequate policies and procedures in place to instruct agency staff on
how to intervene in domestic violence and abuse cases. There should also be
specialist support for victims and their children as well as services for families,
friends and others who may be affected by the death.

The purpose of a DHR is to ensure agencies are responding appropriately
to victims of domestic violence and abuse by offering and putting in place
appropriate support mechanisms, procedures, resources and interventions with
an aim to avoid future incidents of domestic homicide and violence. The DHR
will also assess whether agencies have sufficient and robust procedures and
protocols in place, which were understood and adhered to by their staff.

2.7.5 The Care Act 2014 and Domestic Abuse

The statutory guidance issued under the Care Act 2014[17] states that adult
safeguarding means *'protecting an adult's right to live in safety, free from abuse
and neglect'*. It should not be forgotten that a considerable amount of adult

---

[16] https://www.gov.uk/government/collections/domestic-homicide-review
[17] https://www.gov.uk/government/publications/care-act-statutory-guidance/care-and-support-statutory-guidance#contents

safeguarding work in people's homes relates to the domestic abuse of people with care and support needs. There is a good deal of overlap between safeguarding and domestic abuse procedures. Where domestic abuse has happened this may in some cases require a safeguarding response by the local authority. The Care Act 2014 places a number of duties on local authorities.

For a safeguarding response to be required by the local authority under the Care Act 2014, the individual involved has to meet the following three criteria:

- having care and support needs (whether or not the authority is meeting any of those needs);

- experiencing (or being at risk of) abuse or neglect; and

- being unable to protect themselves because of those needs.

The Care Act states that freedom from abuse and neglect is a key aspect of a person's wellbeing. The Care Act guidance outlines that abuse and neglect can take many forms and can be caused deliberately or unintentionally.

The guidance outlines that the aims of adult safeguarding in the local authority are to:

- Stop abuse or neglect wherever possible;

- Prevent harm and reduce the risk of abuse or neglect to adults with care and support needs;

- Safeguard adults in a way that supports them;

- Promote an approach that concentrates on improving life for the adults concerned;

- Raise public awareness;

- Provide information and support to help people understand the different types of abuse, how to stay safe and what to do to raise a concern about the safety or wellbeing of an adult;

- Address what has caused the abuse or neglect.

For instance, if the above three criteria are satisfied, the local authority will then have a duty to make, or cause to be made, enquiries if it believes the adult in question is experiencing or at risk of abuse or neglect. Such an investigation will determine what action should be taken by the local authority or others (e.g. extra care or support or a change in the way services are provided). If it is discovered that a crime is likely to have been committed the police may be involved.

If you want to learn more about a local authority's role and duties in relation to the Care Act and domestic abuse, the Local Government Association provides guidance in relation to 'Adult safeguarding and domestic abuse – A guide to support practitioners and managers' (Second edition (2015)).[18]

---

[18] http://www.local.gov.uk/c/document_library/get_file?uuid=5928377b-8eb3-4518-84ac-61ea6e19a026&groupId=10180

3.   Training

The Church of England requires domestic abuse training to be undertaken by those who will have roles with survivors and alleged or known perpetrators. This includes all DSAs and pastoral workers and teams.

A modular safeguarding learning and development programme has been created which builds core, generic safeguarding training according to role, and through a person's ministry path, as well as identifying specialist areas of training which will be necessary for some roles. See *Practice Guidance: Safeguarding Training and Development* (2017), available from Church House Publishing or online via www.churchofengland.org/safeguarding

One of the specialist training modules is S3 – Responding to domestic abuse/violence. This specialist training module aims to examine issues relating to domestic abuse, especially for vulnerable groups and children in the context of adult abuse, and how the Church can respond well to this.

By the end of the module / on return to their workplaces, with use of personal notes and module learning resources and to meet prescribed national standards participants will be able to:

- List key statistics and describe possible behaviours relating to domestic abuse;

- Evidence responding appropriately to information about domestic abuse;

- Describe a range of ways to manage risk to adults who are vulnerable and children;

- List and describe referral pathways and the roles of supporting agencies;

- Reflect on the implications of responding well to domestic abuse for traditional Christian teaching about marriage.

The module will explore issues for vulnerable groups and children in the context of adult abuse.

Domestic abuse fact sheet

This fact sheet aims to increase awareness of domestic abuse, the statutory definition of abuse and specialist types of abuse, its prevalence and effects. It provides guidance on how to recognise both victims/survivors and alleged perpetrators. The information is offered as best practice reference material.

1 Definition of domestic abuse

The cross-government definition of domestic abuse (see https://www.gov.uk/guidance/domestic-violence-and-abuse) is: any incident or pattern of incidents of controlling, coercive, threatening behaviour, violence or abuse perpetrated by those aged 16 or over who are, or have been, intimate partners or family members regardless of gender or sexuality. The abuse can encompass, but is not limited to:

- psychological
- physical
- sexual
- financial
- emotional

The Church recognises additional categories of neglect, spiritual and digital abuse.

Examples of all these categories are:

- **psychological/emotional**

For example, shouting; swearing; frightening; blaming; ignoring or humiliating someone; blackmailing them; threatening harm to children or pets if they misbehave; ridiculing every aspect of their appearance and skills; keeping them deliberately short of sleep; being obsessively and irrationally jealous; keeping them isolated from friends and family; threatening suicide or self-harm.

> **Coercive Control** – Section 76 of the Serious Crime Act 2015 created an offence of controlling or coercive behaviour in an intimate or family relationship which occurs when a person repeatedly or continuously engages in behaviour towards another person to whom they are personally connected that is controlling or coercive and that has a serious effect on their victim. Victims who experience coercive and controlling behaviour that stops short of serious physical violence, but amounts to extreme psychological and emotional abuse, can bring their alleged or known perpetrators to justice.

> The offence closes a gap in the law around patterns of controlling or coercive behaviour that occurs during a relationship between intimate partners, former partners who still live together or family members.
>
> Please refer to Appendix 2 'The Legal Context' for more details in relation to this offence.

- **physical**

Causing physical pain or discomfort in any way, for example, hitting; slapping; burning; pushing; restraining; giving too much medication or the wrong medication; assault with everyday implements such as kitchen knives; kicking; biting; punching; shoving; smashing someone's possessions; imprisoning them; or forcing them to use illegal drugs as a way of blackmailing and controlling them.

- **sexual**

For example, forcing someone to take part in any sexual activity without consent, e.g. rape or sexual assault, including marital rape; forcing them or blackmailing them into sexual acts with other people; sexual name calling; imposition of dress codes upon a partner; involvement in the sex trade or pornography; knowingly passing on Sexually Transmitted Infections; controlling access to contraception; sexual exploitation; trafficking.

- **financial**

For example, the illegal or unauthorised use of someone's property, money, pension book or other valuables; forcing them to take out loans; keeping them in poverty; demanding to know every penny they spend; refusing to let them use transport or have money to pay for it.

- **neglect**

Depriving or causing deprivation of basic standards of care as per the Care Act 2014 guidance document section 14. For example, a failure to provide necessary care, assistance, guidance or attention that causes, or is reasonably likely to cause a person physical, mental or emotional harm or substantial damage to or loss of assets.

- **spiritual**

For example, telling someone that God hates them; refusing to let them worship (e.g. not allowing a partner to go to church); using faith as a weapon to control and terrorise them for the perpetrator's personal pleasure or gain; using religious teaching to justify abuse (e.g. 'submit to your husband'), or to compel forgiveness.

- **digital**

For example, the use of technology (e.g. texting and social media) to bully, harass, stalk or intimidate a partner. Though it is perpetrated online, this type of abuse has a strong impact on a victim's real life. For example, the 'revenge porn' offence i.e. disclosing private sexual photographs via digital media with an intention to cause distress.

Domestic abuse may involve areas of risk that are complex and require safeguarding support from specialist agencies. These may include so-called 'honour based violence', forced marriage, female genital mutilation, child to adult abuse and elder abuse (see section 9 below).

2. Who experiences domestic abuse?

Domestic abuse can occur to anyone regardless of age, race, disability, sexuality, class, or income. Most domestic abuse is perpetrated by men against women, but the perpetrator of domestic abuse can be of any gender, and the victim can be of any gender. Victims can be male, although the majority are female, and abuse can occur in same sex relationships, between siblings or by adult children against a parent. Many victims will only disclose that a partner was violent and abusive after leaving a relationship.

- Women are particularly vulnerable to abuse when pregnant or seeking to leave a relationship.

- Older people and disabled people can be particularly vulnerable to domestic abuse.

- Children experience domestic abuse in many ways including through directly intervening to protect one of their parents, being forced to join the adult perpetrator and hearing or witnessing violent attacks or verbal abuse.

- Coercive and controlling behaviour in a domestic abuse situation can be exerted over the whole family so any children suffer as well as the victim.

- Many women come to the UK to work and improve their lives, and many can then become trapped in relationships characterised by abuse with no avenue to seek safety and support.

- The Church of England requires domestic abuse training to be undertaken by those who will have roles with survivors and alleged or known perpetrators. This includes all DSAs and pastoral workers and teams. Domestic abuse happens within the Church; church leaders, members of the clergy, and spouses of clergy have been found to be victims of domestic abuse.

3. Statistics

Domestic abuse statistics for England and Wales

General

- 2 women are killed every week in England and Wales by current or former partners (Office of National Statistics, 2015) – 1 woman killed every 3 days.

- 1 in 4 women in England and Wales will experience domestic violence in their lifetimes and 8% will suffer domestic violence in any given year (Crime Survey of England and Wales, 2013/14).

- 6.5% of domestic violence incidents reported to the police result in a conviction (Women's Aid, 2014).

- 8.2% of women and 4.0% of men reported experiencing any type of domestic abuse in 2014/15. This is equivalent to an estimated 1.3 million female victims and 600,000 male victims (Crime Survey for England and Wales, March 2015).

- Overall, 27.1% of women and 13.2% of men had experienced any domestic abuse since the age of 16, equivalent to an estimated 4.5 million female victims and 2.2 million male victims (Crime Survey for England and Wales, March 2015).

- Domestic violence has a higher rate of repeat victimisation than any other crime (Home Office, July 2002).

- On average, a woman is assaulted 35 times before her first call to the police (Jaffe, 1982).

Children

- 20% of children in the UK have been exposed to domestic abuse (Radford et al. NSPCC, 2011).

- In 90% of domestic violence incidents in family households, children were in the same or the next room (Hughes, 1992).

- 62% of children in households where domestic violence is happening are also directly harmed (Safelives, 2015).

- 1 in 5 teenagers have been physically abused by their boyfriend or girlfriend, with boys much more likely to be the perpetrators (Barter et al. 'Partner exploitation and violence in teenage intimate relationships'. NSPCC and Bristol University, 2009).

Health

- 30% of domestic violence either starts or will intensify during pregnancy (Department of Health report, October 2004).

- Foetal morbidity from violence is more prevalent than gestational diabetes or pre-eclampsia (Friend, 1998).

4. Challenging misconceptions about domestic abuse

Many people will have misconceptions and attitudes about domestic abuse which are incorrect. Here are some common myths about what domestic abuse is and who it affects:

Myth 1: It happens to certain types of people

It can be thought that domestic abuse happens to a certain type of person – based on socio-economic status, religious or cultural backgrounds, or a perception of strength and resilience. This is not the case. Domestic abuse and violence can happen to anyone at any time.

Myth 2: It happens because of…

Domestic abuse is complex, and is not necessarily explained by a single theory. It can be thought that domestic abuse happens because of alcohol abuse, unemployment, child abuse, mental or physical ill health, or other environmental factors. Although these may be contributory factors, abuse happens because an abusive person chooses to behave in a way that enables them to have power and control over another person – excuses and reasons are given to justify abusive behaviour.

Myth 3: A victim can cause a perpetrator to become abusive

Often a perpetrator will tell a victim that they caused them to do it. A victim is never responsible if a perpetrator chooses to behave in an abusive and controlling way.

Myth 4: A victim can fully understand what is happening to them

When someone is in a relationship in which they are subject to abuse they will often feel very confused about what is happening, and they are sometimes not sure that what they are experiencing is abuse.

Myth 5: A victim can choose to leave and if they don't, they are choosing to stay

People ask why victims stay in a situation where they are suffering abuse, and assume that it is easy to leave and to escape the situation and start a new life. This is not the case on a practical and emotional level. A perpetrator of abuse will work to ensure that the victim feels that they cannot cope on their own. Leaving is a very dangerous thing to do. It may also be financially impossible to leave the situation, particularly when there are children. Victims often do not have a choice in leaving and may feel, or be, threatened that if they leave they will be in danger. It may be safer to stay than to leave.

Myth 6: Domestic abuse is about anger

Domestic abuse is choice to act in a controlling way; it is not about being angry and losing control.

Myth 7: Domestic abuse doesn't happen in our church

Domestic abuse happens in every community, including within the Church. With one in four women affected in the UK, it is extremely likely that there will be those in your church who have been affected by domestic abuse.

5. Recognising domestic abuse in adult victims/survivors

It is very difficult to create a definitive list of signs that domestic abuse is happening because abuse can occur on many levels and both victims and alleged or known perpetrators can behave and respond in a range of different ways. The following list of signs of behaviour for victims is not exhaustive, and should not be used as a definitive list but should be used as guidance.

- Has unexplained bruises or injuries;

- Shows signs of feeling suicidal;

- Becomes unusually quiet or withdrawn;

- Has panic attacks;

- Has frequent absences from work or other commitments;

- Wears clothes that conceal even on warm days;

- Stops talking about her/his partner;

- Is anxious about being out or rushes away;

- May never be seen alone, and is always accompanied by their partner;

- May become more isolated, possibly moving away from home, withdrawing from friends and family;

- Goes along with everything their partner says and does;

- Checks in often with their partner to report where they are and what they're doing;

- Receives frequent, harassing phone calls from their partner;

- May have unexplained injuries, and may give other reasons for the injuries which refer to them being accidental.

Survivor view

The abuse went on for six years before I realised that what I was experiencing wasn't just a bad marriage. Everyone says marriage is difficult so at first I thought it was that – our adjustment to married life.

There was pressure to make marriage work and to sacrifice yourself. After all the church says 'till death us do part'. I bent over backwards to make it work.

From the outside most people thought we were the perfect happy couple. But I was walking on eggshells in my own home, never knowing what mood he would be in when he came home.

It was such a lonely time. I didn't think anyone would believe me if I told them what it was really like at home. I was desperate for some hope.

6. Recognising domestic abuse in children

Living in a home where there's domestic abuse is harmful. It can have a serious impact on a child's behaviour and wellbeing. Parents or carers may underestimate the effects of the abuse on their children because they don't see what's happening. Indeed, a child who witnesses domestic abuse could be the subject of a care or supervision order.[19] This is because impairment caused by seeing or hearing the ill treatment of another (e.g. witnessing domestic violence or abuse) is included in the definition of 'harm' in the Children Act 1989.

Domestic abuse can also be a sign that children are suffering another type of abuse or neglect.[20] The effects can last into adulthood. However, once they're in a safer and more stable environment, most children are able to move on from the effects of witnessing domestic abuse.

Younger children who experience and witness domestic abuse may:

- Become aggressive;

- Display anti-social behaviour;

- Become anxious;

- Complain of tummy aches and start to wet the bed;

- They may find it difficult to sleep, have temper tantrums and start to behave as if they are much younger than they are;

- They may also find it difficult to separate from their abused parent when they start nursery or school;

- Children may be clingy, have behavioural difficulties, may be tired and lethargic, and struggle in social settings and at school.

Older children/young people who experience and witness domestic abuse react differently:

- Boys seem to express their distress much more outwardly, for example by becoming aggressive and disobedient. Sometimes, they start to use violence to try and solve problems, and may copy the behaviour they see within the family;

- Older boys may play truant and start to use alcohol or drugs (both of which are a common way of trying to block out disturbing experiences and memories);

- Girls are more likely to keep their distress inside. They may become withdrawn from other people, and become anxious or depressed;

- Girls may think badly of themselves and complain of vague physical symptoms. They are more likely to have an eating disorder, or to harm themselves by taking overdoses or cutting themselves;

---

[19] See section 31 of the Children Act 1989 as amended by section 120 of the Adoption and Children Act 2002

[20] Stanley 2011

- Girls are also more likely to choose an abusive partner themselves;

- They may suffer from depression or anxiety.

Children of any age can develop symptoms of what is called 'Post-traumatic Stress Disorder'. They may get nightmares, flashbacks, become very jumpy, and have headaches and physical pains.

Children dealing with domestic violence and abuse often do badly at school. Their frightening experiences at home make it difficult to concentrate in school, and if they are worried about their abused parent, they may refuse to go to school.

Long-term impact on children and young people

As adults, children who have witnessed violence and abuse are more likely to become involved in a violent and abusive relationship themselves. Children tend to copy the behaviour of their parents. Boys learn from their fathers to be violent to women. Girls learn from their mothers that violence is to be expected, and something you just have to put up with.

However, children don't always repeat the same pattern when they grow up. Many children don't like what they see, and try very hard not to make the same mistakes as their parents. Even so, children from violent and abusive families may grow up feeling anxious and depressed, and find it difficult to get on with other people.

Survivor view (13 years old)

It's only in the last year or so that I began to think that a family could be a good place to be ... a home. I'm the eldest, and I took a lot of my Dad's fury – or just being drunk which is what it often was. I know my Mum wasn't always a saint – she could really wind him up – in fact she does it to me sometimes and then I get terrified that I'll react like him.

Anyway sometimes they would just argue and shout, but then I'd seen what he could do when he loses it. I had to take Mum to hospital once and it was just horrible. In fact I remember being amazed how she looked almost normal when they'd cleaned her up. But seeing it or even worse just hearing it was ... don't know ... I couldn't bear it, and I wanted to kill him. I couldn't I know – even if I was strong enough – so I just used to hold on to the little ones and sort of hide with them till it was over. But it did get so difficult. I didn't want to go home after school, so I'd stay out late sometimes with my mates. Then my Mum started saying I was just like him. That was the worst time ever.

One day my Mum spoke to someone on a helpline. After that, they had a big row and then he left home. Things sort of calmed down, but I was still scared that he would come back or I'd be like him. Then we had this counsellor who talked to my Mum, and me and my sisters together. Somehow it all began to seem better and I felt it was possible to move on.

7. Who are the alleged or known perpetrators of domestic abuse?

Most alleged or known perpetrators of domestic abuse are men. This is partly a reflection of the position of men in our society but may also reflect the potential under-reporting of domestic abuse by men.

- Anyone across the social spectrum can perpetrate domestic abuse – a perpetrator's outward appearance may be outgoing and friendly, and/or very confident; whilst the victim may be withdrawn and considered by many as unfriendly, but a disclosure of domestic abuse by an individual should always be taken seriously.

- There is no excuse for abuse. People who abuse their partners make a choice to do so. Often alcohol, childhood problems (such as a violent/abusive childhood), drugs and mental health are cited as causes of domestic abuse. Whilst they certainly may be factors in the situation the reality is that domestic abuse is caused by a misuse of power by one person over another. Individuals who perpetrate domestic abuse generally do so to get what they want and to gain control.

- Domestic abuse happens within the Church; church leaders, members of the clergy, spouses of clergy and prominent lay members have been found to be alleged or known perpetrators of domestic abuse.

- Seeing change in alleged or known perpetrators is a long-term process. Perpetrator programmes are long-term groups or one to one interventions which challenge the underlying attitudes and beliefs that drive domestic abuse. For more details and the availability of local domestic abuse perpetrator programmes contact Respect (http://respect.uk.net) or the local authority.

8. Recognising alleged or known perpetrators of domestic abuse

Alleged or known perpetrators are very good at hiding their behaviour. The following list of signs of perpetrator behaviour is not exhaustive, and should not be used as a definitive list but should be used as guidance:

- Presents confidently;

- Focuses on themselves and has no empathy with partner;

- Assertively claims victim status;

- Finds no fault in themselves;

- Makes unfounded accusations;

- Puts partner down and portrays partner often as unreasonable or unstable;

- Does not consider the children's experiences;

- Makes disparaging remarks about their partner in public;

- Uses their wedding vows as leverage to keep their partner tied to them – 'you promised...';

- Expresses suspicion about legitimate activities of partner;

- Restricts access to partner's family and friends;

- Recruits others to back them up against their partner;

- Uses inappropriate humour, especially about compliance;

- Tries to engender pity in order to manipulate and recruit colluders;

- Shows changeable behaviour in order to hold onto control;

- Uses scripture to justify behaviour or requests.

9. Specialist types of domestic abuse

9.1   Introduction

Domestic abuse can take several forms and awareness of the wide variety of types of abuse will help us all in identifying abuse and responding appropriately.

Culturally specific forms of abuse such as so-called 'honour' crimes, 'honour' killings, forced marriage, female genital mutilation, the abuse of children and/or women related to 'possession by evil spirits' or 'dowry problems' must be addressed within the framework of domestic abuse. Indeed, the need to protect remains the main imperative, irrespective of the cultural context in which domestic abuse occurs. Such forms of abuse are common across the various religious communities and are often justified by religious and cultural beliefs as a way of maintaining patriarchal power and control. Often the violence or abuse is perpetrated by members of the extended family, with the collusion of others in the community.

9.2   'Honour based' violence

There is no specific 'honour based offence'. The terms 'honour crime', 'honour based violence' or 'izzat' embrace a variety of crimes of violence (mainly but not exclusively against women), including assault, imprisonment and murder, where the person is being punished by their family or their community. They are being punished for actually, or allegedly, undermining what the family or community believes to be the correct code of behaviour.

In transgressing this correct code of behaviour, the person shows that they have not been properly controlled to conform by their family and this is to the 'shame' or 'dishonour' of the family. It can be distinguished from other forms of abuse, as it is often committed with some degree of approval and/or collusion from family and/or community members. Victims may have multiple perpetrators not only in the UK; HBV can be a trigger for a forced marriage.

Transgressions may include an intimate relationship outside of marriage; rejecting a forced marriage; pregnancy outside of marriage; interfaith relationships; seeking divorce and inappropriate dress or make-up.[21]

---

[21] HM Government Multi-agency practice guidelines: Handling cases of Forced Marriage, June 2014

Women and girls are the most common victims of honour based violence; however males can also be victims, sometimes as a consequence of a relationship which is deemed to be inappropriate, if they are gay, have a disability or if they have assisted a victim.

This is not a form of abuse which is perpetrated by men only, sometimes female relatives will support, incite or assist. It is also not unusual for younger relatives to be selected to undertake the abuse as a way to protect senior members of the family or as a way of showing them the potential consequences of dis-honouring the family.

There can be specific risks from family and the wider community in cases of Honour based abuse and forced marriage. It is important that risks to victims are not underestimated or assumed and that those at risk are asked what risks they face and from whom. Guidance for statutory agencies makes reference to the 'one chance rule'. That is, that all professionals working with suspected or actual victims of forced marriage or honour based violence may only have one opportunity to speak to a victim or potential victim and may possibly only have one chance to save a life. If the victim is allowed to walk out of the door without support being offered, that one chance might be wasted.

How to respond to a disclosure of actual or potential honour based violence

HBV cases can involve a variety of complex and sensitive issues that should be handled by a child protection or adult protection specialist. Please contact your DSA and follow the disclosure flowchart (see section 2.1.1), but in addition:

Do

Advise the victim of Karma Nirvana, a UK registered charity that supports victims of honour based abuse and forced marriage. They can be contacted via their helpline 0800 5999247 (9am – 9pm Weekdays & 10am – 4pm Weekends). Karma Nirvana not only provides support to victims but also to those dealing with a case. If possible offer the victim a secure place to make the telephone call and be there to support them if this is what they would like.

Do not

- Send them away;

- Approach members of their family or the community;

- Share information with anyone without the victim's express consent;

- Breach confidentiality – unless there is an imminent risk of serious harm or threat to life of the victim;

- Attempt to be a mediator or encourage mediation, reconciliation, arbitration or family counselling.

9.3　Forced marriage

A forced marriage (FM) is a marriage conducted without the valid consent of one or both parties and where some form of duress is involved (e.g. threats, violence or any other form of coercion). Since 2014, the Anti-Social Behaviour, Crime and Policing Act 2014 makes FM a criminal offence and can result in a sentence of up to 7 years in prison. If you know or have a reasonable suspicion that a FM has taken place then you should report to the police.

There is a clear distinction between a FM and an arranged marriage. In arranged marriages, the families of both spouses take a leading role in arranging the marriage, but the choice of whether or not to accept the arrangement still remains with the prospective spouses. However, in a FM one or both spouses do not consent to the marriage but are coerced into it. The pressure put on people to marry against their will can be physical (including threats, actual physical violence and sexual violence) or emotional and psychological (for example, when someone is made to feel like they're bringing shame on their family). Financial abuse (taking away wages or not giving someone any money) can also be a factor. In the cases of vulnerable adults who lack the capacity to consent to marriage, coercion is not required for a marriage to be forced and any action carried out which causes the victim to enter into a marriage would be considered to be an offence.

Disclosures of FM should not be dismissed as merely a domestic issue – for many people, seeking help from an agency is a last resort and therefore all disclosures of FM should be taken seriously.

How to respond to a disclosure of actual or potential Forced Marriage

Forced marriage cases can involve a variety of complex and sensitive issues that should be handled by a child protection or adult protection specialist. Please contact your DSA and follow the disclosure flowchart (see section 2.1.1), but in addition:

Do

Advise the victim of The Forced Marriage Unit and support them to make contact (via their helpline, 0207 008 0151 (9am – 5pm) or 0207 008 1500 (if outside the office hours (ask for the Global Response Centre)). This unit not only provides support to victims but also to those dealing with a case. If possible offer the victim a secure place to make the telephone call and be there to support them if this is what they would like.

Forced Marriage Protection Order (FMPO)

A FMPO is a civil remedy issued under the Forced Marriage (Civil Protection) Act 2007.

A person can apply for a FMPO if one of the following applies:

● He/she or someone else is being threatened with a forced marriage;

- He/she is in a forced marriage.

The FMPO is designed to protect a person according to his/her individual circumstances, e.g. to stop someone removing him/her from the UK. A FMPO contains such prohibitions, restrictions or requirements and any other terms that the court thinks appropriate. An application for a FMPO can be made by the victim, a person obtaining the court's permission to apply for an order on behalf of the victim, a relevant third party (as specified by the order of the Lord Chancellor) or by the court itself.

An emergency order (an 'ex-parte' or 'without notice' order) can be obtained to protect a person immediately without the individual, against whom the order is being made, being involved in the process.

Remember: call 999 if a person is in immediate danger.

Breach of a FMPO is criminal offence under section 120 of the Anti-Social Behaviour, Crime and Policing Act 2014.

9.4   Female Genital Mutilation (FGM)

Female genital mutilation (FGM) is illegal in the UK and is a form of child abuse. For information with regards to FGM and how the Church should respond to and support victims or potential victims please refer to 'Promoting a Safer Church: The Church of England's Policy for children, young people and adults'.

9.5   Women and girls in black and minority ethnic (BME) communities

Whilst many of the common myths and assumptions about domestic violence and women in the wider society are also applicable to BME women and girls, such women and girls have extra constraining factors to overcome due to their race or ethnicity. These act as barriers within and outside the community. Churches need to be aware of these issues when supporting women from BME communities.

Within some communities, the following can act as additional obstacles:

- tight-knit families and communities where the religious and community leadership is conservative, women have limited public visibility and the incidence of sexual discrimination may be high;

- notions of honour and shame which are strongly held features of family and community existence;

- lack of alternative safe havens, where women are not judged or condemned for leaving violent relationships;

- forced engagement in community mediation and reconciliation processes which have added to the pressures that women are already facing to 'save' their marriage/relationship.

Outside these communities, the following can act as additional obstacles:

- racial discrimination;

- racial violence;

- inability to access services and support due to language difficulties and isolation;

- lack of specialist facilities for minority women;

- the dominance of the 'multicultural approach' which can amount to non-intervention on grounds of respect for 'cultural sensitivity';

- insecure immigration and asylum status.

- For further information please see earlier Appendix 1 sections on 'Honour based violence', forced marriage and female genital mutilation.

In addition the Home Office in partnership with Southwell Black Sisters has produced a helpful leaflet, in several languages, called 'THREE STEPS TO ESCAPING VIOLENCE AGAINST WOMEN AND GIRLS: A guide for black and minority ethnic (BME) women and children'. https://www.gov.uk/government/publications/three-steps-to-escaping-domestic-violence

9.6 Domestic abuse and young people

People in the age group 16–24 are those most at risk of domestic abuse.

The changes to the definition of domestic abuse, to include 16 and 17 year olds, raise awareness that evidence increasingly shows that young people in the 16 to 17 age group can also be victims of domestic abuse.

Domestic abuse is still a 'hidden' issue in our society; and it is even more so for teenagers. This is exacerbated by the fact that adolescents can be more accepting of, and dismissive about, this form of behaviour than adults.

It is important to be aware that cases involving under 18 year olds may include features of domestic abuse, sexual abuse, child sexual exploitation and street gang-related sexual and other violence.

Although some features of teenage relationship abuse are similar to adult domestic abuse, the forms and experience of this issue, as well as the challenges in seeking and providing services, make many of the issues faced by teenagers unique. There are also certain barriers relating to young people's ability to access services. Simply because of their age many young people are unable to access the same levels of support as those over 18.

Many young people will be experiencing multiple risk factors. However, as with abuse in adult relationships, teenage relationship abuse occurs across diverse groups and cultures. Teenage relationship abuse can occur in various forms, including verbal, emotional, physical, sexual, and financial, and the experience may have both immediate and long-term effects on young people. It is sometimes the case that there are unclear parameters between victim and perpetrator which adds to the complexity of cases.

9.7 Same-sex domestic abuse

Domestic abuse occurs in the lesbian, bisexual, gay and transgender community. It is estimated that about 25% of LGBT people suffer through violent or threatening relationships with partners or ex-partners which is about the same rates as in domestic abuse against heterosexual women. As in opposite-gendered couples, the problem is under-reported. Those involved in same-gender abuse are often afraid of revealing their sexual orientation or the nature of their relationship.

There are many parallels between LGBT people's experience of domestic abuse and that of heterosexual women. However, there are a number of aspects that are unique to LGBT domestic abuse:

'Outing' as a method of control – The perpetrator may threaten to 'out' the victim to friends, family, religious communities, co-workers, and others as a method of control. The perpetrator may use the close-knit dynamic of the gay and lesbian community and the lack of support for LGBT people outside the community to further pressure the victim into compliance.

Abuse associated with sexual orientation or gender identity – For many people, their sexual orientation or gender identity becomes associated with the abuse so that they blame the abuse on being lesbian, gay, bisexual or transgender. So they may feel that they are experiencing this abuse because they are lesbian, gay, bisexual or transgender or that if they weren't lesbian, gay, bisexual or transgender that they wouldn't be experiencing it. This can therefore fuel feelings of internalised homo/bi/transphobia.

Domestic abuse isn't well recognised in the LGBT community – There hasn't been much information or discussion in the LGBT communities about domestic abuse. Most information on domestic abuse relates to experiences of heterosexual women. This lack of understanding means that some people may not:

- Believe it happens in LGBT relationships;

- Recognise their experience as domestic abuse if it does happen to them;

- Know how to respond if they see domestic abuse being experienced by their friends.

Confidentiality and isolation within the LGBT communities – LGBT communities are often hidden and can rely on friends and relationships as support within the local community; this is often compounded when living in smaller towns and rural areas and can make it difficult for the abused partner to seek help. They may feel ashamed about the abuse, or their partner may have tried to turn others in the community against them. An abusive partner may isolate their partner from contact with the LGBT community by preventing them from reading any LGBT papers/magazines etc. or attending LGBT venues or events and preventing them seeing friends from within the community. This can be especially true for people in their first same-sex relationship who may not have had much contact with the LGBT community before the relationship began.

For additional information on abuse in same-sex relationships see the websites of LGBT anti-violence charity Galop (http://www.galop.org.uk) which runs the national LGBT Domestic Violence Helpline or Stonewall (http://www.stonewall.org.uk) which provides services for those affected.

9.8 Child and adolescent to parent abuse

Child or adolescent to parent abuse may be referred to as 'adolescent to parent violence (APV)', 'adolescent violence in the home (AVITH)', 'parent abuse', 'child to parent abuse', 'child to parent violence (CPV)', or 'battered parent syndrome'.

It is important to recognise that child or adolescent to parent abuse is likely to involve a *pattern of behaviour*. This can include physical violence from a child or adolescent towards a parent and a number of different types of abusive behaviours, including damage to property, emotional abuse, and economic/financial abuse. Abuse can occur together or separately.

Abusive behaviours can encompass, but are not limited to, humiliating language and threats, belittling a parent, damage to property and stealing from a parent and heightened sexualised behaviours. Patterns of coercive control are often seen, but some families might experience episodes of explosive physical violence from their adolescent with fewer controlling, abusive behaviours.

It is also important to understand the pattern of behaviour in the family as a whole; siblings may also be abused or be abusive. There may be a history of domestic abuse, or current domestic abuse occurring between the parents of the young person.

Domestic abuse is notoriously difficult to identify when it occurs within the family home. This can become even harder if the abuse is child or adolescent to parent abuse. Like other forms of domestic abuse, child to parent abuse is very likely to be under-reported. Many of these families may be facing multiple issues such as substance use, mental health issues and domestic violence. The lack of recognition of this issue means that many families may not recognise that they need support and may feel unable to ask for help due to feeling stigma and shame. There are also often issues of lack of awareness of existing support (notably family support groups); parents not seeing themselves as legitimate recipients of support; lack of knowledge on drugs, alcohol and their effects; an 'it'll never happen to us' mind-set; and a lack of consensus on the best course of action within couples.

It is important to recognise the effects that child or adolescent to parent abuse may have on both the parent and the young person and to establish trust and support for both. It is also important that a young person using abusive behaviour against a parent receives a safeguarding response.

Responding to disclosure of child to adult abuse:

Do

- Remember this is domestic abuse (and general domestic abuse considerations apply);

- Show understanding; consult with a DSA, who will consider whether other referrals need to be made, for example to:

  - Public protection specialists or local policing staff: they may have existing knowledge;

  - Are other children at risk in the house? If so, you will need to make a referral to Children's Services.

Do not

- Assume that this is a parenting issue – the parent is the victim in this situation;

- Joke or make light of the situation;

- Underestimate how difficult it is for the parent to report the incident and for the young person to accept responsibility;

- Wait until something more serious happens before taking action.

9.9   Elder abuse

Abuse of older people is a hidden, and often ignored, problem in society. While the profile of child abuse has been raised in recent years a number of organisations and bodies have been responsible for reminding us of the particular needs and problems that can be associated with older people.

> No standard definition of elder abuse applies within the UK public sector. The term itself has been imported from the USA. It has no legal status and would not be recognised by many older people.
>
> In 1993 Action on Elder Abuse[22] established the following definition of elder abuse. This has been subsequently adopted by the World Health Organisation, is promoted by the International Network for the Prevention of Elder Abuse, and has been variously adopted by countries throughout the World:
>
> > **'A single or repeated act or lack of appropriate action, occurring within any relationship where there is an expectation of trust, which causes harm or distress to an older person'.**
>
> It has at its heart the 'expectation of trust' that an older person may rightly establish with another person, but which is subsequently violated.

---

[22] Action on Elder Abuse is a UK charity established in 1993 (www.elderabuse.org.uk/) by a group of practitioners from health and social care, and by academics and representatives of the voluntary sector who were concerned about the lack of information and assistance for those vulnerable older people who were abused or were at risk of being abused. Today the charity addresses abuse within an older person's own home (whether by family, friends or paid staff), within sheltered housing, and within care homes and hospitals.

Both older men and women can be at risk of being abused. People can be abused in different ways. These include: physical abuse; psychological abuse; financial abuse; sexual abuse; spiritual abuse; neglect; inappropriate use of medication.

Abuse can occur anywhere: for instance, in someone's own home; a carer's home; day care; residential care; a nursing home; hospital.

The perpetrator is usually well-known to the person being abused. They may be: a partner, child or relative; a friend or neighbour; a paid or volunteer care worker; a health or social worker, or other professional. Older people may also be abused by a person they care for.

There are many reasons why abuse occurs and these may vary with each incident. Abuse may range from a spontaneous act of frustration to systematic premeditated assaults on an older person. At home some of the causes would appear to include: poor-quality long-term relationships; a carer's inability to provide the level of care required; a carer with mental or physical health problems. In other settings, abuse may be a symptom of a poorly run establishment. It is likely to occur when staff are: inadequately trained; poorly supervised; have little support from management; or work in isolation.

If you become aware or concerned about someone you know, it is important that you refer the case to your local authority adult social care department.

Appendix 2:

The legal context

You should be aware that, despite your concern, any older person has the right to decline assistance.

Further specialist resources can be found in Appendix 9.

Individuals who are subjected to domestic abuse can seek protection via two possible routes.

The first route a victim can use is by making a complaint to the police, which could result in a criminal prosecution.[23]

Most cases can be categorised as an offence against the person and the police can make arrests for offences such as assault, battery, actual bodily harm, grievous bodily harm or one of a number of sexual offences. They can also make arrests for harassment under the Protection from Harassment Act 1997, which includes a stalking offence (e.g. which could encompass behaviour such as watching or spying on a person; interfering with a person's possessions). A person does not have to be the victim of a physical assault in order to be subjected to harassment (or stalking). This legislation provides both civil and criminal remedies. These include non-harassment and restraining orders.[24] There is also the 'revenge porn' offence contained in section 33 of the Criminal Justice and Courts Act 2015, which creates an offence of disclosing private sexual photographs and films with intent to cause distress, which could equally be viewed, in some cases, as a form of domestic abuse.

A further criminal offence was introduced in 2015 which closed the gap in the law around patterns of controlling or coercive behaviour in an intimate or family relationship (section 76 of the Serious Crime Act 2015). This offence criminalises patterns of coercive behaviour where they are perpetrated against a family member or between individuals who are or used to be in an intimate personal relationship. The offence carries a maximum sentence of 5 years' imprisonment, a fine, or both.

The behaviour, when viewed in isolation, may appear innocuous, but the cumulative effect on a victim may be significant, causing damage and distress. Although there is no statutory definition of controlling of coercive behaviour, the Government has issued statutory guidance under section 77 of the Serious

---

[23] For further information in relation to offences and possible remedies in connection with "Honour Based Violence"; Forced Marriage and Female Genital Mutilation see paragraphs 9.2, 9.3 and 9.4 and Promoting a Safer Church.

[24] Section 12 of the Domestic Violence, Crime and Victims Act 2004 amended the Protection from Harassment Act 1997, to extend the availability of restraining orders to all offences, and also to give the court the power to make a restraining order even when a person has been acquitted, where the court considers it necessary to do so to protect a person from harassment by the defendant

Crime Act 2015. This guidance contains the following cross-Government definitions of 'controlling behaviour' and 'coercive behaviour':

'Controlling behaviour is: A range of acts designed to make a person subordinate and/or dependent by isolating them from sources of support, exploiting their resources and capacities for personal gain, depriving them of the means needed for independence, resistance and escape and regulating their everyday behaviour.'

'Coercive behaviour is: A continuing act or pattern of acts of assault, threats, humiliation and intimidation or other abuse that is used to harm, punish, or frighten their victim.'

The guidance also gives a non-exhaustive list of the types of behaviour that may be associated with coercion or control.[25] A person investigating offences with regard to controlling or coercive behaviour must have regard to this guidance.

The second route a victim can use is to pursue directly a claim for damages and/or other remedies through the civil courts.

It is possible to pursue a civil claim where the conduct does not constitute a criminal offence or there is insufficient evidence to convict or where a person does not want to involve the police. The standard of proof in civil courts is lower than in criminal courts, (i.e. 'balance of probabilities' rather than 'beyond all reasonable doubt'). A civil claim for domestic abuse would usually take the form of an action for negligence, battery, or trespass to the person, depending on the circumstances of the case. Examples of remedies in the civil court are damages, injunctions, non-molestation orders and occupation orders under the Family Law Act 1996 (as amended by Part 1 of the Domestic Violence Crime and Victims Act 2004).

Domestic Violence Disclosure Scheme

Since March 2014 there has been the Domestic Violence Disclosure Scheme (colloquially known as 'Clare's law'), which contains two specific rights. That is a 'right to ask', which allows an individual to ask police to check whether a new or existing partner has a violent past, and a 'right to know', which enables an agency (e.g. a statutory agency or a charity) or an individual to ask the police to release information concerning an individual being at risk of domestic violence. The police will consider whether to release the information to the individual involved or to the person that is best placed to protect that individual.

Anyone can apply for a disclosure by visiting their local police station or calling 101. The police will ask for an overview of your concerns and take your contact details. You may be invited to a face to face discussion where you will require two forms of ID. The police will undertake a risk assessment and will make a disclosure to the person affected if they believe that abuse is likely. They will then help any potential victim to put together a safety plan. You may not hear the outcome of your request if the police do not deem this to be necessary.

---

[25] Controlling or Coercive Behaviour in an Intimate or Family Relationship – Statutory Guidance Framework (December 2015) https://www.gov.uk/government/uploads/system/uploads/attachment_data/file/482528/Controlling_or_coercive_behaviour_-_statutory_guidance.pdf

Government guidance in relation to domestic violence and abuse can be found on the website listed below, in particular there is guidance on the Domestic Violence Disclosure Scheme, as well as further information about how to report domestic abuse and where to get help: https://www.gov.uk/guidance/domestic-violence-and-abuse

Domestic Violence Notices and Orders

The initial period of response to domestic abuse is critical. Domestic Violence Protection Notices and Orders (DVPN and DVPO) are part of a scheme introduced in March 2014 that provides protection to victims in the immediate aftermath of domestic violence. The scheme comprises an initial temporary notice (the DVPN), authorised by a senior police officer and issued to the perpetrator by the police, followed by a DVPO that can last from 14 to 28 days, imposed at the magistrates' court. Under the DVPO scheme, the police and magistrates can, in the immediate aftermath of a domestic violence incident, ban the alleged perpetrator from the family home or victim's residence or to have any contact with the victim for up to 28 days. This is important as, often due to lack of evidence or the victim's reluctance to pursue a prosecution, the perpetrator may not be charged and therefore cannot be bailed with any conditions to stay away. DVPOs are designed to help victims who may otherwise have had to flee their home, giving them time to access support and consider their options.

Restraining orders

Restraining orders can be made on conviction or acquittal for any criminal offence. These orders are intended to be preventative and protective. The guiding principle is that there must be a need for the order to protect a person or persons. The test to be applied by the court before making an order is whether an order is necessary to protect the persons named in it from harassment or conduct that will put them in fear of violence. This necessitates an evaluation by the court of the evidence before it. It will require the court to determine whether there is sufficient evidence in front of it to enable it to form a view that an order is necessary. Restraining orders are civil behaviour orders and therefore the standard of proof is a civil one.

Other civil court orders

There are also two main orders which the courts can make. These are called the Non-Molestation Order and an Occupation Order. Secular legal aid may be available for an application for a Non-Molestation Order and/or Occupation Order. This is means and merit tested. An Occupation Order controls who can live in a property. It can also restrict the respondent from entering a certain area. If you do not feel safe living with the respondent and you have left because of violence or intimidation and want to return without the respondent being there, the order you would apply for is an Occupation Order. A Non-Molestation

Order prevents the respondent from using or threatening violence against you (and if applicable your child/children) or intimidating, harassing or pestering you. This is to ensure the health, safety and wellbeing of yourself (and if applicable your child/children). A breach of a Non-Molestation Order is an arrestable offence and now carries a maximum sentence of 5 years imprisonment. A breach of an Occupation Order is not a criminal offence but will be regarded as 'contempt of court' in a civil court. That said, a power of arrest can be attached to an Occupation Order, which means that an individual can be arrested if the Occupation Order is breached.

APPENDIX 3:

Theology

The table below lists some scriptures that have been used unhelpfully with regard to victims of domestic abuse together with how the same scriptures could be applied helpfully.

SCRIPTURE	UNHELPFUL APPLICATION	HELPFUL APPLICATION
Submission 'Wives submit yourselves to your own husbands as you do to the Lord' *Ephesians 5.22*	**Obedience** The woman must obey her partner **Not submitting causes abuse** If a man abuses his partner it is because she is not being submissive enough.	**Mutual submission** The previous verse 5.21 says 'submit to one another' and 5.22 must be read in light of the mutual submission we should be giving to one another. To submit does not mean to obey, it means to choose to place oneself under another. **Submission is a choice** Submission cannot be forced, it must be chosen. Not submitting can never justify abuse.
Headship 'For the husband is the head of the wife as Christ is the head of the church, his body of which he is the Saviour' *Ephesians 5.23*	**The asserting of power** The man is the head; therefore he has all the power and the right to assert it. **Superiority** Headship means being superior and having the right to take more than give.	**The laying down of power** The example given of headship is of Christ's headship of the Church. When Christ came to earth, he gave up all his heavenly power for his bride, the Church. The original Greek word used for head in this passage is Kephale. This word means the head of a river or the source of the river. It does not imply superiority.
Rulership 'To the woman he said, "… Your desire will be for your husband and he will rule over you."' *Genesis 3.16*	**Rulership: a right** God determined men should rule their wives, therefore that is how it should be.	**Rulership: a result** A consequence of sin is that a man will rule over his wife, it is not God's best plan for humanity, before the Fall men and women were equal.

SCRIPTURE	UNHELPFUL APPLICATION	HELPFUL APPLICATION
Creation of Woman "The Lord God said, "it is not good for the man to be alone. I will make a helper suitable for him." *Genesis 2.18*	**Inferior** To help means to serve, this verse shows that God created women to serve men and suggests they are inferior to them.	**Equal** The word 'helper', here referring to women, most often refers to God in the Old Testament usage (e.g. 1 Samuel 7.12; Psalm 121.1–2). Therefore there is no suggestion of female inferiority.
Forgiveness 'And forgive us our debts, as we have forgiven our debtors.' *Matthew 6.12*	**Disregard** Forgiving someone should mean disregarding what they have done and maintaining the same relationship with them regardless of whether they change.	**Consequences** Sin has consequences and forgiving does not remove those consequences. Forgiveness is a process and must not nullify the consequences of abuse or mean that the situation must continue as it always has. Women should not have to stay in an abusive situation in order to forgive their partner.
Original Sin 'When the woman saw that the fruit of the tree was good for food and pleasing to the eye, and also desirable for gaining wisdom, she took some and ate it. She also gave some to her husband, who was with her, and he ate it.' *Genesis 3.6*	**Sin: women are weaker** Eve took the fruit, and gave some to her husband; this shows women are weaker and more likely to be sinful.	**Sin: equal responsibility** Man and woman were both participants in the Fall: Adam was no less to blame than Eve. Romans 5.12–21: 'Therefore, just as sin entered the world through one man, and death through sin, and in this way death came to all people, because all sinned.'
Divorce 'But I tell you that anyone who divorces his wife, except for sexual immorality, causes her to become an adulteress …' *Matthew 5.32*	**Contract** Marriage is a contract and the person who cancels the contract, i.e. files for divorce is the one who is responsible. Therefore if a woman divorces a man for abusing her, she is at fault, not him.	**Covenant** Marriage is a covenant; divorce is the breaking of that covenant. When a man chooses to be abusive, he breaks the covenant. If his wife chooses to divorce him, she is making public his breaking of the covenant, not going against what the Bible says about divorce.
Suffering 'In all this you greatly rejoice, though now for a little while you may have had to suffer grief in all kinds of trials.' *1 Peter 1.6*	**Accept** Women should accept abuse and use the suffering as an opportunity to grow their faith.	**Refute** By staying in a relationship where she is subject to abuse a woman is risking being murdered. When Jesus was tempted to risk his life, he said 'It is also written: "Do not put the Lord your God to the test"' (Matthew 4.7). God wanted abused women to be safe and protected.

Diocesan Statement on domestic abuse

Diocese of XXX Domestic Abuse Policy

All forms of domestic abuse are wrong and must stop. We are committed to promoting and supporting safer environments which:

- ensure that all people feel welcomed, respected and safe from abuse;

- work to protect those experiencing domestic abuse;

- recognise equality amongst people and within relationships;

- refuse to condone any form of abuse;

- enable and encourage concerns to be raised and responded to openly and consistently.

We recognise that:

- all forms of domestic abuse cause damage to the survivor and express an imbalance of power in the relationship;

- all survivors (regardless of age, disability, gender, racial heritage, religious belief, sexual orientation or identity) have the right to equal protection from all types of harm or abuse;

- domestic abuse can occur in all communities;

- domestic abuse may be a single incident, but is usually a systematic repeated pattern which escalates in severity and frequency;

- domestic abuse, if witnessed or overheard by a child, is a form of abuse by the perpetrator of the abusive behaviour;

- working in partnership with children, adults and other agencies is essential in promoting the welfare of any child or adult suffering abuse.

We will respond to domestic abuse:

In all our activities by –

- valuing, listening to and respecting both survivors and alleged or known perpetrators of domestic abuse, whilst appreciating the need to ensure a distance is kept between the two and refusing to condone the perpetration or continuation of any form of abuse.

In our publicity by –

- raising awareness about other agencies, support services, resources and expertise, through providing information in public and women-only areas of relevance to survivors, children and alleged or known perpetrators of domestic abuse.

When concerns are raised by –

- ensuring that those who have experienced abuse can find safety and informed help;

- working with the appropriate statutory bodies during an investigation into domestic abuse, including when allegations are made against a member of the church community.

In our care by –

- ensuring that informed and appropriate pastoral care is offered to any child, young person or adult who has suffered abuse;

- identifying and outlining the appropriate relationship of those with pastoral care responsibilities with both survivors and alleged or known perpetrators of domestic abuse.

We are committed to reviewing our policy and procedures regularly.

APPENDIX 5:

Parish statement on domestic abuse

Parish of _____

Policy for Responding to Domestic Abuse

All forms of domestic abuse are wrong and must stop. We are committed to promoting and supporting environments which:

- ensure that all people feel welcomed, respected and safe from abuse;

- protect those vulnerable to domestic abuse from actual or potential harm;

- recognise equality amongst people and within relationships;

- enable and encourage concerns to be raised and responded to appropriately and consistently.

We recognise that:

- all forms of domestic abuse cause damage to the survivor and express an imbalance of power in the relationship;

- all survivors (regardless of age, disability, gender, racial heritage, religious belief, sexual orientation or identity) have the right to equal protection from all types of harm or abuse;

- domestic abuse can occur in all communities;

- domestic abuse may be a single incident, but is usually a systematic, repeated pattern which escalates in severity and frequency;

- domestic abuse, if witnessed or overheard by a child, is a form of abuse by the perpetrator of the abusive behaviour;

- working in partnership with children, adults and other agencies is essential in promoting the welfare of any child or adult suffering abuse.

We will endeavour to respond to domestic abuse by:

In all our activities –

- valuing, listening to and respecting both survivors and alleged or known perpetrators of domestic abuse.

In our publicity –

- raising awareness about other agencies, support services, resources and expertise, through providing information in public and women-only areas of relevance to survivors, children and alleged or known perpetrators of domestic abuse.

When concerns are raised –

- ensuring that those who have experienced abuse can find safety and informed help;

- working with the appropriate statutory bodies during an investigation into domestic abuse, including when allegations are made against a member of the church community.

In our care –

- ensuring that informed and appropriate pastoral care is offered to any child, young person or adult who has suffered abuse;

- identifying and outlining the appropriate relationship of those with pastoral care responsibilities with both survivors and alleged or known perpetrators of domestic abuse.

If you have any concerns or need to talk to any one please contact ....

APPENDIX 6:

Draft Safety and Exit plan[26]

Step 1:   I CAN USE SOME OR ALL OF THE FOLLOWING STRATEGIES

A. If I decide to leave, I will _____
_____.

(Practise how to get out safely. What doors, windows, stairwells or fire escapes would you use?)

B. I can keep my purse and car keys ready and put them
_____ (place) in order to leave quickly.

C. I can tell _____ about the violence and request they call the police if they hear suspicious noises coming from my house.

D. I can teach my children how to use the telephone to contact the police and the fire department.

E. I will use _____ as my code for my children or my friends so they can call for help.

F. If I have to leave my home, I will go _____
(Decide this even if you don't think there will be a next time). If I cannot go to the location above, then I can go to
_____ or
_____.

G. I can also teach some of these strategies to some/all of my children.

H. When I expect we are going to have an argument, I will try to move to a space that is lowest risk, such as _____
_____. (Try to avoid arguments in the bathroom, garage, kitchen, near weapons or in rooms without access to an outside door.)

I. I will use my judgment and intuition. If the situation is very serious, I can give my partner what he/she wants to calm him/her down. I have to protect myself until I/we are out of danger.

---

[26] Source: Elaine Rose, DSA, Diocese of Canterbury

Step 2:   SAFETY WHEN PREPARING TO LEAVE

Leaving must be done with a careful plan in order to increase safety. Perpetrators often strike back when they believe that the person they are abusing is leaving the relationship.

I can use some or all the following safety strategies:

A.   I will leave money and an extra set of keys with _____ so that I can leave quickly.

B.   I will keep copies of important papers and documents or an extra set of keys at _____.

C.   I will open a savings account by _____, to increase my independence.

D.   Other things I can do to increase my independence include: _____ _____

E.   The domestic violence programme's hot line telephone number is _____ and I can seek shelter by calling this hot line.

F.   I can keep change for phone calls on me at all times. I understand that if I use my mobile, the following month the telephone bill will tell my perpetrator the numbers that I called after I left. I could get a 'pay as you go' phone. There are no bills and all communication would be confidential.

G.   I will check with _____ and _____ to see who would be able to let me stay with them or lend me some money in an emergency.

H.   I can leave extra clothes with_____.

I.   I will sit down and review my safety plan every _____ in order to plan the safest way to leave the residence.

   _____ (domestic violence advocate or friend) has agreed to help me review this plan.

J.   I will rehearse my escape plan and, as appropriate, practise it with my children.

Step 3:   SAFETY IN MY OWN RESIDENCE

There are many things that a person can do to increase her safety in her own residence. It may be impossible to do everything at once, but safety measures can be added step by step.

Safety measures I can use include:

A.   I can change the locks on my doors and windows as soon as possible.

B.   I can replace wooden doors with steel/metal doors.

C.   I can install security systems including additional locks, window bars, poles to wedge against doors, an electronic system, etc.

D.   I can purchase rope ladders to be used for escape from second floor windows.

E.   I can install smoke detectors and purchase fire extinguishers for each floor in my house/apartment.

F.   I can install an outside lighting system that lights up when a person is coming close to my house.

G.   I will teach my children how to use the telephone to make a reverse charge call to me and to _____ (friend/ other) or get them a mobile phone in the event that my partner takes the children.

H.   I will tell people who take care of my children which people have permission to pick up my children and that my partner is not permitted to do so. The people I will inform about pick-up permission include:

_____ (school)

_____ (day care staff)

_____ (Sunday School teacher)

APPENDIX 7:

Confidentiality and data protection

Confidentiality

If in doubt about whether to disclose information please contact the DSA and Diocesan Registrar for guidance.

Although information relating to domestic abuse may be given in confidence, it should be made clear from the outset, to the person providing the information, that in certain situations such information may be passed to a third party (e.g. the police).

If domestic abuse information has been received in confidence, the provider of the information should be encouraged, in the first instance, to disclose it to the relevant authorities him or herself or alternatively, consent should be sought to make a disclosure. Seeking consent or encouraging a person to make a disclosure should always be the first option but there may be circumstances where consent is refused or cannot otherwise be obtained or is just inappropriate because it places a person at increased risk or might prejudice an ongoing investigation. In such cases, a recipient of the information may still be able to share the information without consent if it can be justified in the public interest. Such a public interest can arise in a wide number of situations, for instance, to protect a person, notably a child, from significant harm or prevent, help, detect or prosecute a criminal offence.

The key factors in deciding whether or not to share confidential information without consent are necessity and proportionality, i.e. whether the proposed sharing is likely to make an effective contribution to preventing any risk and whether the public interest in sharing the information overrides the confidentiality. In making the decision, a person should weigh up what are the risks if the information is shared against what are the risks if it is not shared and make a decision based on his or her professional judgement, or by seeking advice from the DSA and the Diocesan Registrar. It may be necessary to make a disclosure without consent, for example, when a disclosure would be likely to assist in the prevention, detection or prosecution of a serious crime, especially a crime of violence. Indeed, when a victim of domestic abuse refuses to contact the police, disclosure will be justified if children remain at risk, for example.

Data protection

Under the Data Protection Act 1998, sensitive personal data includes information which relates to a person's physical or mental health, sexual life or to the commission or alleged commission of an offence. The 1998 Act restricts the use of such information, including disclosure to third parties, without the explicit consent of the data subject (i.e. the individual to whom the information relates). Nevertheless, there are certain instances, under data protection legislation,[27] where such information can be shared without a data subject's consent provided that it is in the substantial public interest, for instance this includes:

- if it is necessary for the purposes of the prevention or detection of any unlawful act; or

- to protect members of the public against dishonesty, malpractice or other seriously improper conduct; or

- it is necessary for the discharge of any function which is designed for the provision of confidential counselling, advice, support or any other service;

- and seeking consent would prejudice the purposes for which the information is sought.

If you are unsure whether or not you can disclose personal and/or confidential information to a relevant third party you should speak to the DSA and the Diocesan Registrar.

Storage of confidential records

All confidential records (whether or not they contain personal data) should be stored safely and securely in line with Safeguarding Records: Joint Practice Guidance for the Church of England and the Methodist Church (2015).[28]

---

[27] Data Protection (Processing of Sensitive Personal Data) Order 2000

[28] https://www.churchofengland.org/media/2254792/safeguarding%20joint%20practice%20guidance%20-%20safeguarding%20records.pdf

APPENDIX 8:

Marriage preparation: Recommended good practice

Marriage preparation offers an opportunity to challenge inappropriate behaviour and assumptions about domination, control or abuse, while making it clear that some degree of conflict within an intimate relationship is natural and healthy, if dealt with appropriately.

The principles of understanding humanity (female and male) as made in God's image and of equal worth; of equality amongst people and within relationships; not condoning any form of abuse, should underpin any marriage preparation offered by the Church. Some theological ideas such as headship and submission models of men and women have been expressed in the liturgy in the past in the different promises expressed by the man and the woman. However, a promise to obey was in the past part of different standards or expectations of women and men within marriage, e.g. the fact that women had no standing in law until 1926. A mutuality expressed through the marriage which encourages partners to be themselves rather than sticking to gendered roles offers a better opportunity for both partners to grow and flourish in the relationship than does a differentiated model, in which one partner takes responsibility for the other's growth, but not vice versa.

Given the high incidence of domestic abuse within marriage, we recommend that clergy and lay people who offer marriage and wedding preparation should have attended some training on issues of domestic abuse. It is important that there is a clear understanding amongst those who offer marriage preparation that domestic abuse is always unacceptable and that domestic abuse breaks the sanctity of marriage.

The subjects regularly dealt with when preparing couples for marriage, e.g. communication, conflict and in particular 'How do you deal with your anger?' offer an opportunity for couples to discuss together how their parents dealt with anger, rows and conflict or how the couple might have dealt with these in previous relationships. Sometimes those who have experienced domestic abuse as children have a very idealised view of marriage.

It is possible that those working with couples hoping to marry may become aware or suspect that abuse is taking place or may take place between the partners. This is always a difficult area to deal with and illustrates the need for training for people involved in this work, but one or more of the following ideas might help in such a situation.

The facilitator might include a statement at the beginning of the 'course' or conversation and again before dealing with a subject such as 'marital conflict' or anger. The following, which may need amending depending on the circumstances, is an example of a form of words that might be appropriate:

'When we think about relationships in general and our own in particular, there is always a chance that issues may be raised that touch us in a way that leaves us feeling disturbed, uncomfortable or anxious. If this happens you may wish to speak to one of us today more privately or to seek help from a counsellor or other helping organisation.'

If a domestic abuse issue is raised directly or indirectly by one of the couple, the facilitator should not pursue it in the presence of the other: this could be highly dangerous. They may need to find a way to give the person a chance to say more in private, with the object of encouraging them to get one-to-one help from a competent person or organisation.

APPENDIX 9:

Resources

Women's Aid

Provides services for women and children who have been affected by the experience of domestic violence, rape and sexual abuse.

0808 2000 247
www.womensaid.org.uk

Refuge

Refuge is the national charity which provides a wide range of specialist domestic violence services to women and children experiencing domestic violence.

0808 2000 247
www.refuge.org.uk

Rape Crisis

Rape Crisis Centres offer a range of services for women and girls who have been raped or experienced another form of sexual violence.

0808 802 9999
www.rapecrisis.org.uk

National Domestic Violence Helpline

The Freephone 24 Hour National Domestic Violence Helpline run in partnership between Women's Aid and Refuge.

0808 2000 247

National Centre for Domestic Violence

The National Centre for Domestic Violence (NCDV) provides a free, fast, emergency injunction service to survivors of domestic violence.

24 hour helpline: 0800 970 2070
www.ncdv.org.uk

NSPCC ChildLine

Free, confidential service for young people up to the age of 19. Get help and advice about a wide range of issues, talk to a counsellor online, send ChildLine an email or post on the message boards.

0800 1111
www.childline.org.uk

NSPCC Helpline

Free helpline service for anyone with concerns about a child's safety and wellbeing, even one in their own home. You can speak to a NSPCC counsellor 24 hours a day, 365 days a year. Advice and support is provided for parents and carers and consultations with professionals are offered. We will listen to your concerns, offer advice and support and can take action on your behalf if a child is in danger.

0808 800 5000
www.nspcc.org.uk/what-you-can-do/report-abuse/

Galop

Galop gives advice and support to LGBT people who have experienced hate crime, sexual violence and domestic abuse.

LGBT domestic violence helpline: 0800 999 5428

London LGBT Casework Service: 0207 704 2040
www.galop.org.uk/

Respect

The Respect phone line is a confidential helpline offering advice, information and support to help you stop being violent and abusive to your partner.

0808 802 4040
www.respectphoneline.org.uk
www.respect.uk.net

Samaritans

A 24-hour helpline for any person in emotional distress.

116 123
www.samaritans.org

SafeLives

(formerly Co-ordinated Action against Domestic Abuse (CAADA))

SafeLives is a national charity supporting a strong multi-agency response to domestic abuse. It provides practical help to support professionals and organisations working with domestic abuse victims, with the aim of protecting the highest risk victims and their children – those at risk of murder or serious harm.

0117 403 3220
http://www.safelives.org.uk/

Unfortunately SafeLives does not provide direct support or advice to victims of domestic violence. However, if you are experiencing domestic abuse or are supporting someone who is in that situation, immediate help is available via the National Domestic Violence Helpline.

Resources related to children and young people

Home Office resources regarding adolescent to parent abuse:

The Home Office has produced an information guide on adolescent to parent abuse:

https://www.gov.uk/government/uploads/system/uploads/attachment_data/file/420963/APVA.pdf

Holes in the Wall

A blog run by a professional social worker which provides updates on research, practice and policymaking developments – also available on Twitter (@HelenBonnick).

http://holesinthewall.co.uk/

RESPECT

A membership association for domestic abuse prevention programmes and integrated support services. The Young People's Service is a sub-site which offers regular conferences and training for practitioners who are working with young people who use violence in close relationships (including against parents). 020 7549 0578

http://respect.uk.net/work/respect-young-peoples-service/

Resources regarding teenage relationship abuse

The Home Office has produced a guide to help consider how the extension to the definition of domestic abuse may impact on working with 16–17 year olds.

https://www.gov.uk/government/uploads/system/uploads/attachment_data/file/142701/guide-on-definition-of-dv.pdf

The Home Office Teenage Relationship Abuse Campaign includes information and resources for schools.

www.homeoffice.gov.uk/crime/violence-against-women-girls/teenage-relationship-abuse/

This is Abuse site. Includes films, support information, young people's message board and FAQs.

http://thisisabuse.direct.gov.uk/

AVA

A national second-tier organisation providing training and consultancy on teenage relationship abuse as well as all other forms of violence against women and girls.

www.avaproject.org.uk

Barnardos

Barnardos is the largest provider of child sexual exploitation support services in the UK. Staffed by qualified professionals, these services provide a safe and confidential environment where young people can go for help, advice and support. Specialist training is also provided to professionals so they know what signs to look out for. 0208 550 8822

www.barnardos.org.uk/

Resources for women in black and minority ethnic communities

Southall Black Sisters

Southall Black Sisters is a not-for-profit organisation set up in 1979 to meet the needs of black (Asian and African-Caribbean) and minority ethnic women.

Helpline Tel. 0208 571 0800
Monday, Wednesday, Friday 9:30am – 4:30pm
http://www.southallblacksisters.org.uk/
Southall Black Sisters, 21 Avenue Road, Southall, Middlesex, UB1 3BL

Resources regarding Honour based violence

Karma Nirvana

Karma Nirvana supports that who suffer or are at risk of honour based abuse or forced marriage.

0800 5999 247 (9am – 9pm Weekdays & 10am – 4pm Weekends)
http://www.karmanirvana.org.uk

Forced Marriage Unit

The Government's Forced Marriage Unit (FMU) is dedicated both to preventing British nationals being forced into marriage overseas and to assisting anyone in the UK faced with the prospect of being forced into a marriage. If you are worried that you might be forced into a marriage or are worried about someone else who may be you should contact FMU on 020 7008 0151 (9am – 5pm) or 0207 008 1500 (if outside the office hours (ask for the Global Response Centre)).

www.gov.uk/forced-marriage

Resources specifically for men

The Men's Advice Line

A confidential helpline for men experiencing domestic violence from
a partner or ex-partner (or from other family members).

0808 801 0327 (Monday – Friday 9am–5pm)
www.mensadviceline.org.uk

Mankind Initiative

Support for male victims of domestic abuse and domestic violence

01823 334 244 (weekdays 10am to 4pm)
www.mankind.org.uk

Christian resources

Restored

Restored is an international Christian alliance working to end violence.
against women and to transform relationships.

http://www.restoredrelationships.org/

RAVE

RAVE is an initiative that seeks to bring knowledge and social action
together to assist families of faith impacted by abuse.

http://www.theraveproject.org

Hidden Hurt

Hidden Hurt is designed to help understand the dynamics of relationships
where abuse is taking place, the different forms abuse can take, its effect
on both direct victims (i.e. person being abused) and indirect victims (i.e.
children living in a house where abuse occurs), specific issues facing the
Christian abuse victim, and helpful links and telephone numbers inside the UK.

http://www.hiddenhurt.co.uk

Faith Trust Institute

A US-based multi-faith organisation working to end sexual and domestic
violence.

http://www.faithtrustinstitute.org/

Spark

Spark works to engage communication and communities to prevent and respond to Violence Against Women and Gender Justice. It provides specialist consultancy supporting domestic abuse work.

http://www.sparkequip.org/

Broken Rites

Broken Rites is an international group offering mutual support and information to separated and divorced spouses/partners of clergy, ministers and Church Army Officers.

http://www.brokenrites.org/

Eve

Eve (formerly Nene Valley Christian Family Refuge) run a family refuge in Northamptonshire and provide training on domestic abuse prevention and response.

http://www.eveda.org.uk/

Resources on elder abuse

Action on Elder Abuse

Elder Abuse Response helpline: 0808 808 8141

http://www.elderabuse.org.uk

General guidance in relation to domestic violence and abuse

Home Office guidance

Information regarding domestic violence and abuse, including links to further material on the new definition of domestic abuse; coercive and controlling behaviour; Domestic Violence Disclosure scheme; Domestic Violence Protection Notices and Orders; Domestic Homicide Reviews (DHR); Independent Domestic Violence Advisors (IDVAs) and MARACs.

https://www.gov.uk/guidance/domestic-violence-and-abuse

Violence against women and girls

In 2016, the Government published its Violence Against Women and Girls (VAWG) Strategy for this Parliament. There is a lot of information contained on the website detailed below which relates to this strategy including FGM; forced marriage and various other policy and strategy documents.

https://www.gov.uk/government/policies/violence-against-women-and-girls

Controlling or coercive behaviour in an intimate or family relationship (Home Office, Dec. 2015)

https://www.gov.uk/government/uploads/system/uploads/attachment_data/file/482528/Controlling_or_coercive_behaviour_-_statutory_guidance.pdf

Resources for training and raising awareness

A selection of church resources:

Jennifer Beresford, *Creating Confidence in Women*, SPCK, 1998.

Domestic Abuse and the Methodist Church: Taking Action, Methodist Publishing House, 2005. Includes theology, prayer cards and draft good practice. Tel. 01733 325002.

Enduring the Silence: CD-ROM resource pack produced by Diocese of Chester, Church House, Lower Lane, Aldford, Chester, CH3 6HP.

Out of the Shadows: Steps towards ending violence – a community-based approach: a Mothers' Union resource pack for use by trained facilitators for work with groups on violence including domestic abuse. http://www.themothersunion.org

Shattered Love . . . Broken Lives . . .: a domestic violence resource pack and CD from the Domestic Violence Task Group of Churches Together in the Merseyside Region. Tel. 0151 709 0125.

'What is this place?' Churches Together in England, 2004. Six studies that follow the journey a woman experiencing violence may make, from recognition of her situation to making a new beginning. Available from: Edith Steele, Churches Together in England, 27 Tavistock Square, London, WC1H 9HH. Tel. 020 7529 8132. Email: Edith.Steele@CTE.org.uk